The
Guitar Principles Path: Level One

Chords & Rhythm

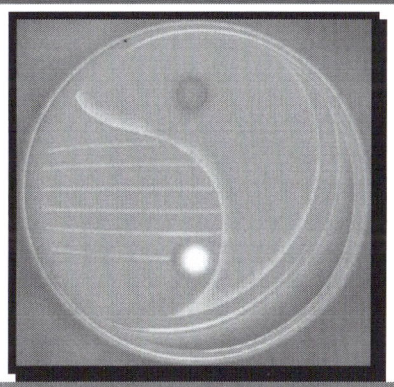

Jamie Andreas

Guitar Principles, Inc.
Las Vegas, Nevada

Publisher:
Guitar Principles, Inc.
2657 Windmill Parkway
Suite #232
Henderson, Nevada 89074
United States of America

Author: Jamie Andreas
Photos & Design: Geraldine Rapetti

Copyright©2002 Guitar Principles, Inc. All rights reserved.
ISBN#978-0-9755285-3-2

Guitar Principles, Inc. has the exclusive rights to reproduce this work, to prepare derivative works from this work, to distribute this work, to publicly perform and give instruction of this work, and to publicly display this work.

All rights reserved. This publication, including all text, photographs and graphics, may not be reproduced, or transmitted, in part, or in full, in any form or by any means, including, but not limited to electronic, mechanical, photo copying, Xeroxing, scanning, posting on Forums, the Worldwide Web, recording, or otherwise, without the prior written permission of Guitar Principles, Inc.

guitar PRINCIPLES™

www.guitarprinciples.com

TABLE OF CONTENTS

THE GUITAR PRINCIPLES PATH: LEVEL ONE - CHORDS

Preface	3

The GuitarPrinciples Path: Chords One
Introduction	6
Playing & Singing Three Blind Mice	7

The GuitarPrinciples Path: Chords Two
Getting Into The Full G Chord	9

The GuitarPrinciples Path: Chords Three
Changing From G Major to E Minor	13

The GuitarPrinciples Path: Chords Four
Changing From E Minor to C Major	16

The GuitarPrinciples Path: Chords Five
Changing From G Major to D Major and C to A Minor	20

THE GUITARPRINCIPLES PATH: LEVEL ONE - RHYTHM

The GuitarPrinciples Path: Rhythm One
The Purpose of This Course	32
The Definitions of the Basic Elements of Music: Notes & Beats	33
Measuring Out Time to Sound	34
Lesson Review	37

The GuitarPrinciples Path: Rhythm Two

Dividing the Beat: Using Counting Symbols	39
The Parts of The Beat	39
The Use of Counting Symbols	40
Lesson Review	43

The GuitarPrinciples Path: Rhythm Three

The Proportionate Relationship of Note Values	44
The Time Signature	47
Lesson Review	51

The GuitarPrinciples Path: Rhythm Four

Strumming Rhythm Patterns Written in Music Notation	52
Exercises and Review	58

The GuitarPrinciples Path: Rhythm Five

Exercises and Review	59

The GuitarPrinciples Path: Rhythm Six

Ties, Dots, Rests, and Syncopation	62
Ties	62
Dots	63
Rests: Notating Silence	67
Syncopation	68
Lesson Review	71

The GuitarPrinciples Path: Rhythm Seven

Sixteenth Notes	72

PREFACE

"The Principles of Correct Practice" for guitar was written in response to the all too obvious lack of a comprehensive approach to learning the guitar that really achieves its intended result: the creation of a real guitar player. It is not obvious if one looks at the millions of guitar methods out there, but it becomes obvious as soon as one looks at the millions of people who own these books, and still cannot make any progress on the guitar!

This was of course my belief when I wrote "The Principles", and it was the undeniable conclusion of thirty years of teaching the guitar, all styles, to all types of students. It was clear that only the talented survived. The vast majority who try do not learn to play, and most that do, even the talented, do so often with severe handicaps to future growth, especially growth into the highest levels of playing ability.

After thousands of book sales, and thousands of testimonials, many of which appear on the GuitarPrinciples.com Website, it is clear that my belief was well founded. However, it is very important to understand <u>why</u> the existing material, (all the wonderful instructional material out there), <u>does not</u> end up at its intended destination: actual playing ability in the guitar student's fingers.

It is because the musical material, that students are given, and the approach to learning it, is incomplete, right from the beginning. <u>The truly important dynamics of the "body learning process" we call "playing the guitar" are not taught, and so practice is often more harmful than helpful.</u> It must be seen that the mechanical operations of the body necessary to playing the guitar are very complex, and <u>all parts of the complex system must be included in a holistic way, right from the beginning of training.</u> A student simply cannot be allowed to develop the fingers while at the same time holding the upper extremity muscles tense in the shoulder, back and chest. And, they always do!

Method books usually make the major mistake of training guitarists from a musical standpoint, instead of the more primary physical standpoint. There is no getting around the fact that playing the guitar is first and foremost, a physical activity. If there are problems in that area, there are going to be problems in the musical area, if the musical area has even been able to develop. It makes no sense if a student can read all the notes in the first position, but is severely locked up with physical tension while doing so. That student is headed for frustration and heartache.

"The Principles" have provided the answer to this "tunnel vision" approach to learning to play the guitar.

In a similar way, the type of musical material that students are given as they go through development as guitarists, is usually dangerously unsystematic. Chords, for instance, are taught in either a random fashion, as they are called for in the teaching of random songs, or, again, from a musical, rather than physical, consideration. So, the chords in the key of C may be taught first, because C is the "first" key, even though those chords, especially the F chord, is very difficult for a relatively new player, or may be impossible to attempt without creating excessive tension. Or, chords may be learned in whatever order they are needed for the "song of the week", as we wander from song to song, by ourselves, or in lessons.

While this haphazard approach to learning music may be fine for an already developed player, it is deadly to the beginner. At the very least, it slows down progress. At worst, it will prevent learning altogether. A systematic, step by step approach is best-an approach that progresses from one technical achievement to another, each one building upon the last- and <u>all</u> of it teaching the fundamental principles of guitar technique along the way.

This is the aim of "The GuitarPrinciples Path: Level One". It will provide that structure so necessary to the beginning student. <u>Excursions into other musical material can be more safely undertaken once the foundation has been established.</u>

It has always been my contention that the student should be enabled to create a musical experience for themselves as soon as possible, and that means as soon as the basics of mechanical functioning have been covered, and the building of solid technique is underway.

"The Principles" serves the purpose of building that solid technique, "The Guitar Principles Path: Level One- Chords & Rhythm" will bring that first musical experience to the student, while at the same time building on, and expanding upon, the technical foundation begun in "The Principles".

"The Path: Level One" is in two parts: Chords and Rhythm. In the section on chords, we begin with the chords in the key of G. They are the easiest to learn, and even they should be learned in an order that is dictated by physical considerations first, then musical ones. There's time enough for playing all the music in the world once we can actually get our fingers to do what we want!

But we don't have to wait to play music, as you will see. In the chord section of **"The Path: Level One"**, we learn chords in a way that makes it possible to avoid the biggest pitfall that all "chord learners" fall into, the one that makes them say "I've been playing guitar for six months. I know lots of chords, but I can't switch them smoothly enough to play a song".

We begin by learning a chord that anyone can do, and a song that needs only one chord. We then move on to a full G chord, and instead of learning a C or D chord next (as would usually be done), we learn to switch smoothly into an E minor chord, because that is easier to do. We will also use this chord change to learn some very important principles of left hand functioning on the guitar, principles that will be a powerful part of your technique throughout your playing lifetime: left hand movement "with support" and "without support". These concepts are directly related to what is being learned and reinforced in **"The Principles"** and by practicing the "Foundation Exercises" therein.

The other half of **"The Path: Level One"** is a treatment of the subject of rhythm. Because of the highly inadequate presentation of this vital element of music, this subject is depressingly impenetrable to the vast majority of guitar students, unless they are lucky enough to have an excellent teacher who is going to make sure they have a firm understanding, or they are attending a professional musical education institution.

There is no getting around the fact that a firm grasp of the subject of rhythm notation, even in its fundamentals, requires a degree of effort. We must put all the "fun stuff" down once in a while and do some real "head work" here, but it must be done. Even if a guitar player decides not to learn how to read music, they must still understand rhythm, and rhythm notation.

So, the course is going to provide all the missing pieces necessary to understanding this subject. Concepts are explained in a most fundamental fashion, and everything that I have found to be missing in existing material, I have provided here.

Taken together, the two parts of "The Guitar Principles Path: Level One, Chords & Rhythm", will provide the next firm addition to the foundation established in "The Principles of Correct Practice For Guitar", one that can be relied upon to allow continuous upward growth in abilities, and understandings as a guitarist, and musician.

THE GUITARPRINCIPLES PATH: CHORDS ONE

Introduction

These lessons for the beginner, to be used along with The "Principles of Correct Practice for Guitar", are designed to teach the student the rudiments of learning chords on guitar.

This means not only the best way to manipulate the fingers into the complex "shapes" demanded by each chord, but also how to *get* from one shape to another. This will enable the student to make music in the manner most natural for guitar players: learning to play and switch chords, and provide the harmonic background for singing, or other melodic accompaniment.

It is important to understand that "The Path: Level One" <u>can and should be used by experienced players as well,</u> if they have reason to be believe that there are serious flaws in their left hand chord changing abilities (which is often the case). Experienced players will discover that the technical insights included here for beginners are most often not part of their own knowledge base concerning guitar technique. They will find a greatly expanded ability to solve their own more advanced left hand "challenges" by applying "The Principles" of left hand movement shown in these "beginner" lessons.

Before using "The Path: Level One", study of "The Principles" should have progressed to the point where the "Understandings" presented in the first two chapters have been studied, and are being applied to the Exercises. Most importantly, the Left Hand Exercises in Chapter Four should be underway, at least in no-tempo fashion.

Training of the right arm and hand should have begun using the "Right Hand String Shifting Exercise", along with application of the instructions for correct holding and use of the pick.

Also, the essential subject of rhythm should begin along with the lessons on chords. This will be achieved by studying "The Path: Level One", and applying the physical skills of changing chords with the mental understanding of rhythm notation. So, the student should study both parts of the book at the same time, both "Chords" and "Rhythm".

In terms of the mental aspect of practice, the need for great attention, and the understanding of how to do adequate no-tempo practice (so that tension is not locked into the body during practice) are the pre-requisites for working with "The Guitar Principles Path: Level One".

The Requirements for Effective Use of "The Path : Level One" Lessons:

- Familiarity and understanding of Chapters 1 & 2 in "The Principles of Correct Practice For Guitar".
- Development of the left hand with the "Foundation Exercises" in Chapter Four of "The Principles".
- Development of the right hand with the <u>"Right Hand String Shifting Exercise"</u>.
- Concurrent study of "The Path: Level One- Rhythm".
- Ability to meet the mental requirements of correct practice.

Exercise 1: Playing & Singing 3 Blind Mice With One Chord, Doing a Quarter Note Down Strum

Instructions: Place the ring finger on the third fret of the first string. Begin to tap your foot, and count out four beats to "set the beat" in your mind and body. Continue tapping and counting while playing.

NOTE: If you are comfortable using the full G chord (see p.10), feel free to do so.

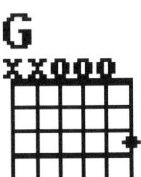

The easy G Chord: Strum only four strings. Leave out strings marked "X".

Goal One: Ability to play the whole song while tapping the foot and knowing where you are in the music. (Each section of four beats is called a measure.)

Goal Two: Ability to sing the song to your playing as described in Goal One. (It doesn't matter how awful your voice is. Grunt if you want to, as long as it is in time with the music).

Special Note: Please appreciate that the coordination required to have the arm and hand strum the steady beat continuously WHILE the brain also monitors the vocal mechanism as it produces the correct rhythm of the words, is QUITE SOPHISTICATED. In other words, the arm and the voice are doing two very different things rhythmically. They often get "tangled up". The arm will stop its steady beat, and start to copy the voice. This must not happen. If it does, back up, try again with more concentration, one measure at a time.

For instance, in measure two, the voice is silent on beat four, while the strum continues. In measure five, the voice sings many syllables inside of the beat, as in "after the" on the second beat. So, this simple song can be quite a challenge for some beginners.

IMPORTANT: You must be able to SING, PLAY and TAP YOUR FOOT completely and perfectly through this song. The ability to do all three of these things together is a VITAL SKILL we must develop right from the beginning. DO NOT go any further until these skills are developed. If you have trouble putting these three things together, then eliminate one of the pieces and put the other two pieces together first. The way to do this is to just hold the guitar on your lap, tap your foot to a steady beat, and SING the words while the foot is going.

INSTRUCTIONS: Practice tapping the foot and strumming the easy G chord, and singing the song "in your head". Then, try tapping the foot, strumming the chord, and humming the tune.

Finally, try all three again, tapping the foot, strumming the chord, and singing the words.

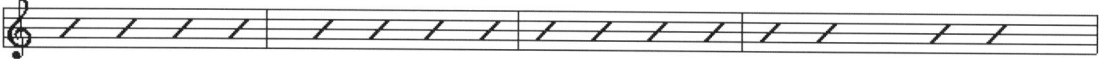

Three Blind Mice   Three Blind Mice   see how they   run

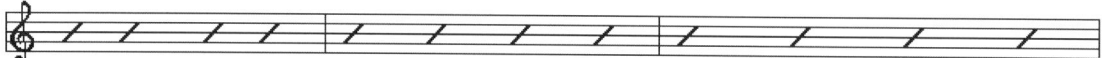

see how they run   they all ran after the farmers wife, who cut off their tails with a carving   knife, you

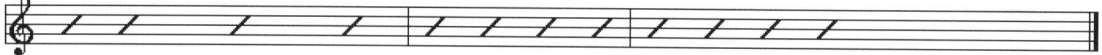

never saw such a sight in your life as   3 Blind Mice,   3 Blind Mice

THE GUITARPRINCIPLES PATH : CHORDS TWO

At this point, it is assumed that you are working with the "Foundation Exercises" from "The Principles", especially the ones in Chapter Four which develop the left hand. The most important thing to develop now is the stretch and strength in the left hand fingers.

However, there is more to it than that. You must, at the same time be applying the "Understandings" of <u>Muscle Memory</u> and <u>Sympathetic Tension</u> as you practice. This means that you must realize that any excess tension you allow to be present in the upper body while practicing the "Foundation Exercises" (or anything) will REMAIN in the all important muscles that control the movement of the upper arm.

Such excess tension will make changing smoothly from chord to chord difficult or impossible, even if the fingers are developing stretch and strength. So, <u>always include an awareness of the upper body while practicing,</u> and train those muscles to be relaxed while they do their job of supporting your arm position, and moving the arm.

Most importantly, be aware of the tension that develops in the upper arm and shoulder when you begin to move the fingers from one chord position to another. USE NO TEMPO PRACTICE, BE AWARE OF YOUR BREATHING AND FOCUS ON THE PHYSICAL SENSATIONS AND MAINTAIN MAXIMUM RELAXATION WHILE MOVING.

Getting Into the Full G Chord

Our goal now is to use our developing ability to operate our fingers in a relaxed way. We are going to use this ability to get into a few new positions on the neck of the guitar. We are going to learn five chords, G, Em, C, D, and Am. We are going to learn these chords, and, most importantly, how to change from one to another smoothly, strumming a steady rhythm.

Once this is accomplished, we will be able to play hundreds of different songs (limited, however, to the key of G). From there, we will have a base from which to conquer other chords and other keys.

We are going to work with these chords, learning to change them smoothly, and applying "The Principles" to our practice. The first challenge is getting into the full G chord in a relaxed way. If you force your fingers into it, and tense your whole body and stop breathing while holding the chord, we are not going to get much further!

Follow these instructions:

Raise your left arm and hand and bring the hand into position down at the 3rd fret, 6th string. We are going to place the 2nd finger down, but you must make sure your arm is relaxed as the hand comes to the neck. You should follow all directions given in "The Principles" for the "Balloon Exercise" in Chapter Four.

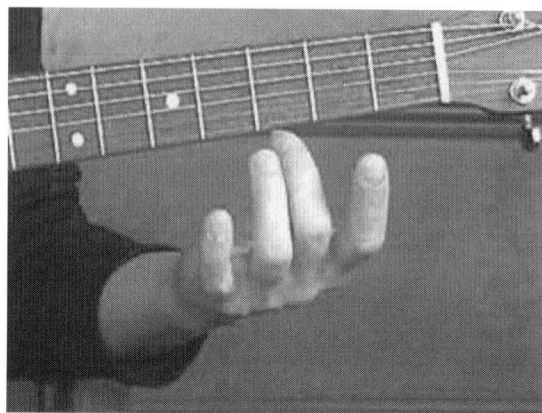

Again, as in the "Balloon Exercise", we are going to place a light, relaxed 2nd finger on the 6th string, which is the first note of the G chord we will place down. After you touch the string with the finger, FLAP it, up and down to make sure it is light and relaxed. WATCH THE OTHER FINGERS AS YOU DO SO, ESPECIALLY THE 3RD FINGER. KEEP THEM AS RELAXED AS POSSIBLE.

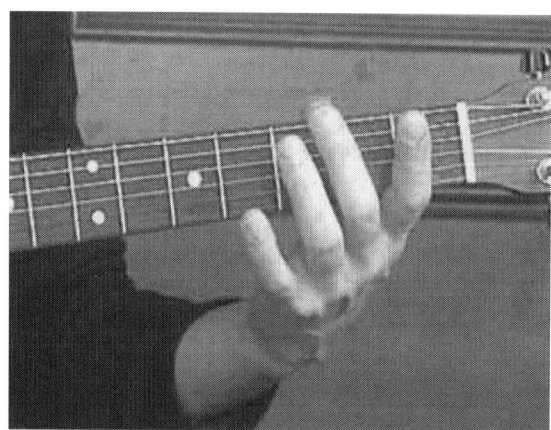

Notice that in doing the G chord, we do not place the 2nd finger down on its tip, or with the distal (tip) joint bent, as we do in many other playing situations, such as scales. Instead, we "overlap" the string a bit with the fingertip. This is because, when the 3rd finger goes down next on the 1st string, it would pull the 2nd off its string if it were straight down on the tip.

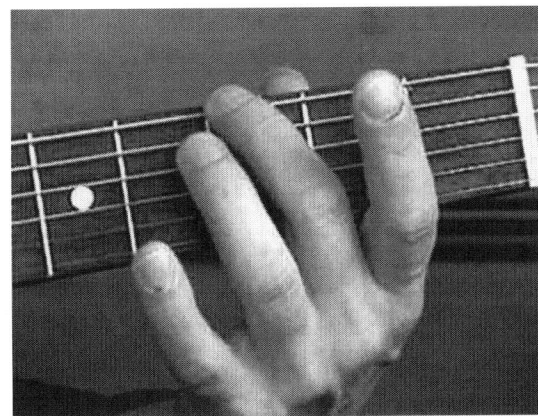

Now, the big job! Moving the 3rd finger to the 1st string, 3rd fret, while keeping the 2nd finger in place, and staying relaxed while doing so. For many people, this is where it all starts to go wrong. They unknowingly allow many muscles in the upper arm, shoulder, and side of the abdomen to tense while they make the effort with the 3rd finger, and they reinforce this every time they practice.

All those muscles are trained to be tense while the fingers are moved into various chords. Then, the student will wonder why they can't change smoothly from chord to chord during a song!

With these understandings in mind, do the following (you now have a light 2nd finger down, as in the picture above. It is not even pressing the string to the fret).

While breathing and focusing on staying as relaxed as possible, begin to bend the 3rd finger toward the 1st string. Do this "No Tempo", stopping frequently to observe the other fingers, other parts of your body, and your breathing. As you do this, you will probably need to move the elbow out a bit from the body, to give the hand a little more "angle" to the neck of the guitar. This gives the 3rd finger a little more room.

You must keep re-establishing relaxation as you move. Do not underestimate the complexity of what you are doing. You are keeping the 2nd finger EXTENDED while you are asking the 3rd finger to perform the opposite motion of FLEXION as it goes to the 1st string. Any time the left hand fingers perform this CONTRARY MOTION, it produces a degree of stress in the muscles, depending on your level of development. In the beginning, it can be quite a bit of stress. If you work properly with it, day by day, it will improve, and begin to feel easier.

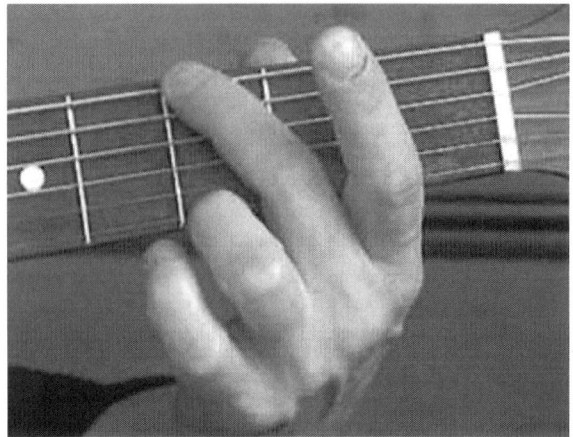

This is how your hand should look after successfully getting the 3rd finger in place. Notice that the 3rd finger DOES go down straight on the tip, with the distal joint quite bent. If you feel tense, use "Posing", breathe, and relax. (Get rid of the rock in your shoulder!)

Slowly bend the 1st finger down onto the 2nd fret, 5th string, also bending at the distal joint.

Voila!! You are doing a full G Chord.

Strum with a pick or your thumb, and if your guitar is in tune you will hear a beautiful sound!

THE GUITARPRINCIPLES PATH: CHORDS THREE

Changing From G Major To E Minor

Step 1- Here we are where we left off, with the Full G chord down. You should be relaxed in position, with a heavy arm (Chapter 4 in "The Principles"), meaning the shoulder is relaxed, and the weight of the arm is conducted through the fingers and onto the strings.

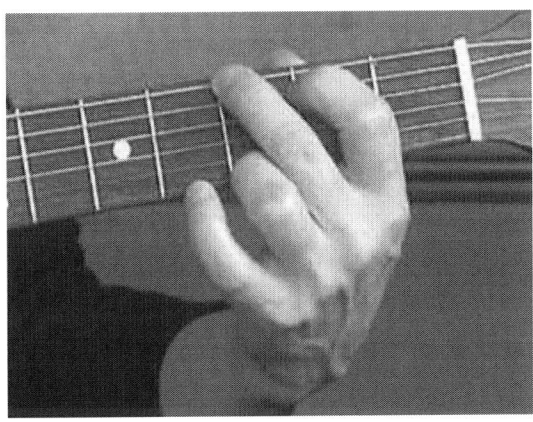

Step 2- Here we release the 2nd and 3rd finger, allowing them to become light and float over the 4th string. We keep the 1st finger down, with all the weight of the arm coming through it.

Step 3- Now, we float the light 2nd finger over the 4th string, 2nd fret. You will need to move the elbow out a bit to allow the 2nd finger to position itself just behind the 2nd fret. Notice the 1st finger is a bit further away from the fret than the 2nd is. This is okay, and a natural consequence of the anatomy of the hand. Just make sure the notes come out clearly. Pick them individually to make sure they don't "buzz".

Touch the string with the fingertip, straight on the tip, with the distal joint very bent, as in the picture. Allow the finger to become firm, and let the arm weight come through.

You are now doing the E minor chord. Strum each string one at a time, and make sure all the notes ring clear. If not, you are probably blocking them by leaning the finger into the string. You must straighten the distal joint more. Remember to relax with every effort.

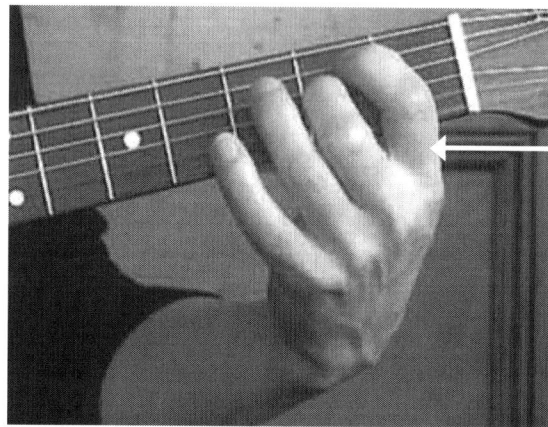

Keep a space between the hand and guitar here!

Completed E Minor chord

Practice Routine for Learning Chord Changes

In order to master this chord change (and all other chord changes), and be able to play it smoothly and in rhythm when playing an actual song, you must practice it correctly, according to "The Principles". That means using the "Basic Practice Approach" and your metronome as follows:

Do Step 1 as written in "The Principles". Step 1 of the "Basic Practice Approach" says: "Review and increase your understanding of what you are about to do, and how you are going to do it." For us now, this means re-reading all the instructions given for doing this chord change. Any detail you forget is going to mean more trouble for you.

Do Step 2 as written in "The Principles". Do five repetitions of the change, "NO TEMPO" and watching your fingers. Use "Posing" also. Then, do another five repetitions.

Do Step 3 as written in **"The Principles"**. On Step 3, where we move to slow tempo from "no tempo", use <u>eight clicks to perform the movement, instead of four.</u>

This gives you eight full seconds to make the change. We need this extra time in order to pay the profound attention needed to manipulate all the fingers WHILE minimizing all body tension, ESPECIALLY the shoulder area. This approach, using eight clicks instead of four, has proven to be extremely effective with students I have trained.

IMPORTANT: Make sure you spread out the movement over the entire length of the eight clicks. Don't for instance, squeeze the movement into the first four clicks and end up in the new chord by click five! You don't get extra points for finishing your work early! Take the full eight beats, and spread the movement out evenly, undoing tension knots as you go.

Continue on to 80 bpm, but take eight clicks again. Then do 100 at eight clicks. From there, resume the "Basic Practice Approach" as written, going to four clicks at 60.

Continue daily work this way, until you have reached 60 at one click per beat without arm and shoulder tension occurring. When the change is able to be done at this speed, try the Exercise below, learning it at eight beats per strum, and working it up to one strum per beat at 60. Repeat it over and over.

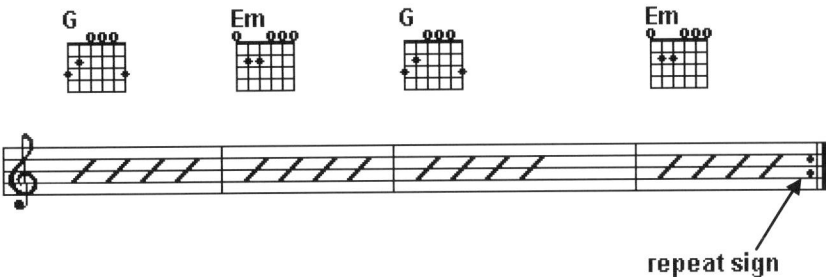

The result of all of this is that you will be able to play a song and get through the changes smoothly. You won't have to stop and hesitate before every change, which is what happens to most beginners.

NOTE: If you don't have a metronome, GET ONE! In the meantime, make sure you take a full eight seconds for the change, AFTER doing "No Tempo Practice", which means extreme slow motion, with no beat.

THE GUITARPRINCIPLES PATH: CHORDS FOUR

Changing From E minor to C major

Preparation for move from E minor to C major:

Keep a space of about a ½ inch here.

Here we are beginning to move out of the E minor chord. When we are in the E minor chord, the arm weight is coming through both the 1st and 2nd fingers. THE 3RD FINGER IS AWAY FROM THE 2ND, AND AS RELAXED AS POSSIBLE. DON'T SQUEEZE IT AGAINST THE 2ND.

E minor chord

And remember this very important thing. <u>As you move, do not allow the hand to come in closer to the neck.</u> This often tends to happen at the base of the index finger (see picture above). This is because the muscles that would otherwise be holding the hand out from the neck do not want to work when they are undeveloped and weak, and the hand wants to come in to the neck to relieve the strain on these muscles. So keep about a half-inch of space between hand and guitar here, BUT STAY AS RELAXED AS YOU CAN THROUGHOUT YOUR ENTIRE SHOULDER AND ARM. If your skin touches the neck it's wrong.

Moving to the C major chord:

Now, we make the move following these steps:

1) Place your attention on your entire arm, breath, and make sure you keep breathing! Allow your 1st finger to become light, and feel the weight of your arm go into the 2nd finger. This is a

nice balanced position for the hand, since the thumb is directly behind the middle finger, which, obviously, is in the center of the hand!

2) Look at your hand in a mirror as you begin to do two things at once: swing your 3rd finger into position for the C chord, at the 5th string 3rd fret (finger extension), Gently bend your 1st finger into position, pulling it to the 2nd string, 1st fret (finger flexion). This is contrary motion of adjacent fingers.

Beginning to Move from E minor to C

You must focus intensely here throughout the arm to keep relaxed during this move. "Posing" and breathing are required here.

As you make this move, your elbow should move toward you slightly. Just make sure your shoulder DROPS and relaxes as the 3rd finger makes its move, and that you stay relaxed after the 1st finger is in position. At this point is where the hand may want to come in toward the neck, losing the space between the hand and guitar. Don't let this happen.

Also, make sure you watch your 4th finger as you move. Do not allow it to tense and stick up (very common). Relax from your shoulder to your fingertip.

The Full C chord

Here is the completed, full C chord. Notice these things:

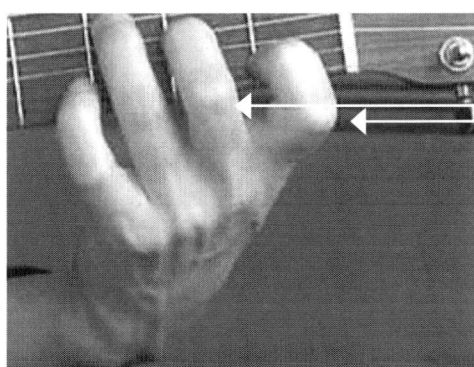

Distal joints are bent. Keep a ½ inch space.

There is a space between all fingers.
The 4th finger is relaxed and pointed toward the fretboard.
The distal (tip) joints are all bent, the 1st finger is bent the most.
The thumb is not visible; it is squarely behind the neck balancing the hand.

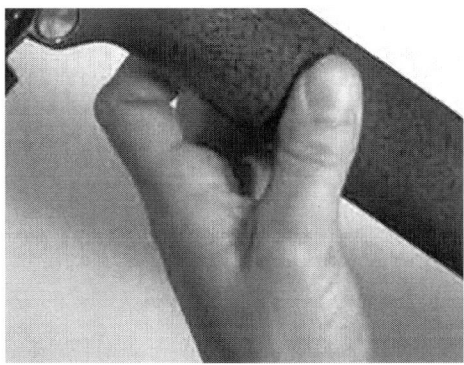

Thumb squarely behind the neck during C Chord

DOING IT WRONG!

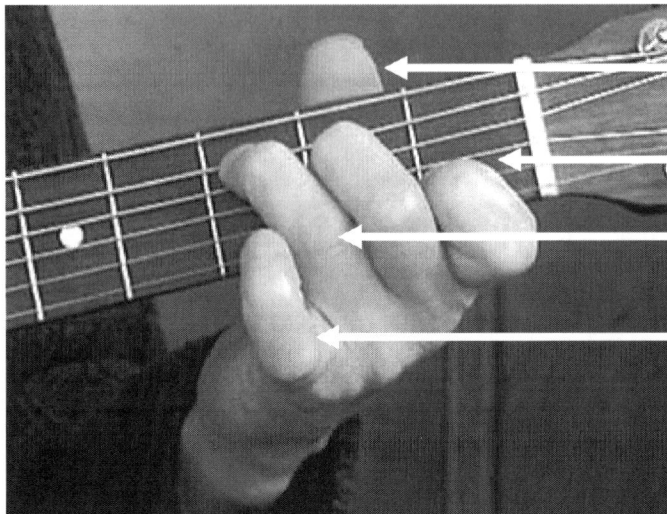

Thumb sticking up, should be behind neck.

No space at base of index finger.

3rd finger squeezing against 2nd.

4th finger sticking up with tension.

C chord done wrong

We might call this a "lazy" C chord. You will see this often. I will have my hand like this for "easy" playing, but never for anything technically demanding.

This position *can* work, but it limits the mobility of the other fingers. For beginners, it is sometimes impossible to get into this position AND clear the strings. The index will frequently block the sound of the first string, touching it and preventing it from ringing freely.

Notice how the fingers are close together and touching. In this picture, I am staying relaxed enough not to cause trouble. Very often, a student will "squeeze" the fingers together, causing muffled strings and other problems.

Understand that even though you may see experienced players use this position, you should have as your goal in practicing the form given as the "correct" one. Learning the correct form will benefit your hand in many other important ways for left hand functioning. Then, you can be "lazy" with the C chord when you want to be!

Learning to change from E minor to C major

Use the Practice Routine for learning chord changes.

Applied Song: Eleanor Rigby

Now, you are ready to use the chord changes, Em to C in a song, "Eleanor Rigby", by the Beatles. The chords of the song have been simplified to only Em and C. The song will sound fine with just these chords, and simplifying it this way will allow us to focus on the most important goal: being able to coordinate steady strumming, smooth chord changes, and singing.

Learn the song first with steady quarter note strums, four to the measure. Then, do the eighth note strum given.

Note: On the Coordination of Strumming and Singing

One of the most difficult aspects of coordinating strumming and singing is dealing with syncopated melody lines being sung against a strum that is keeping to the steady downbeat.

In this song, as in most pop songs, there is a great amount of syncopation in the melody. (see page 65). This means that many of the syllables being sung fall on the upbeat. This is hard to do, especially for beginners. The difficulty of having to sing syllables on the upbeat (when the foot is up) often makes it impossible for the student to learn to sing and play the song.

So, to avoid that problem, and as a preliminary step to singing a song with syncopation, we will first learn the song putting those syllables on the downbeat. We will simplify the melody by putting most of the syllables of the words ON the beat (on the downbeat), instead of OFF the beat (on the upbeat).

This will make the song sound a little "stiff", but will enable you to get a handle on it. After that, you will be able to sing and play with the syncopation in the melody. However, if you were to try to do that first, you would very possibly have lots of trouble.

Of course, if your natural sense of rhythm allows, feel free to go right for the syncopated melody.

For those using the simplified melody, the numbers under the words show the syllable to be singing on each beat.

Also, realize that even though the strum lines in the song are not spaced evenly, you strum them evenly. They are spaced unevenly in order to more closely match the words.

The GuitarPrinciples Path: Level One- Chords & Rhythm
Chords Five

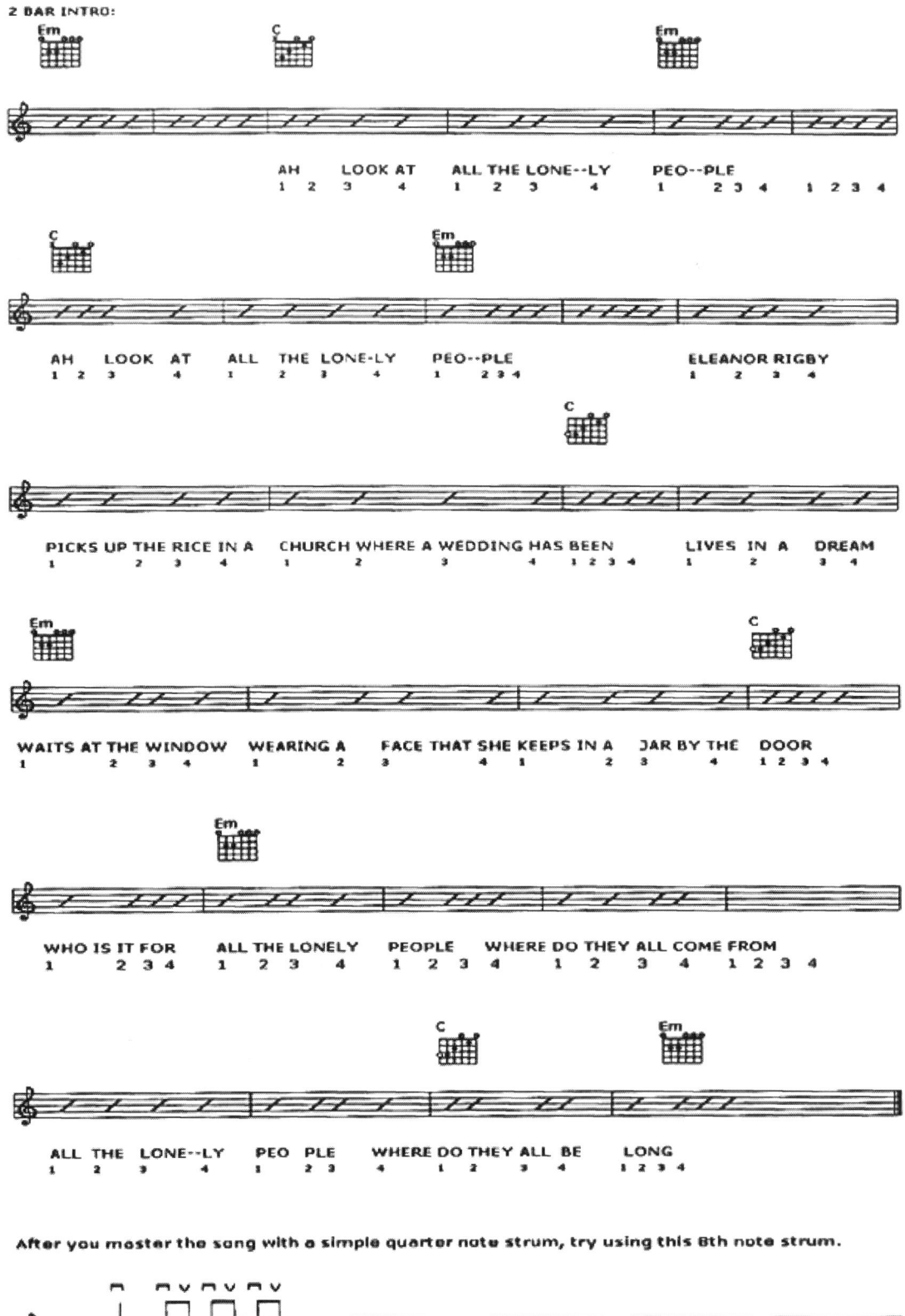

THE GUITARPRINCIPLES PATH: CHORDS FIVE

Changing From G Major to D Major and C to A Minor

The Two Ways of Changing Chords: With Support/ Without Support

As we have seen in the previous **"The GuitarPrinciples Path: Level One"** lessons, it is best to learn to switch between our first position chords by using a finger that is common to both chords as a "pivot" point to move from, which provides "support" for the arm, hand and fingers during their movements.

Players familiar with **"The Principles"** should realize that this means the "heavy arm" is maintained during these changes. We leave certain fingers in place, allowing the arm weight to be directed through the fingers, and allowing the large muscles of the shoulder, and left side of the upper body to stay much more relaxed because they are not being used to support the arm fully. In addition, the arm weight helps us do our work; getting the strings to the frets.

This is best in the beginning. It orients the hand and other fingers to know where they are. In addition, it teaches economy of motion (making as little movement as possible in our playing) right from the beginning. It is also a good idea in the beginning because the fingers, being relatively undeveloped, do not yet have the strength, flexibility and control they need to do these movements easily without support.

Once there has been progress in doing chord changes this way, with support, it is time to start developing another way of changing chords which is very useful, and often necessary: making the changes without support. If a beginner tries to learn chord changes without support first, as often happens, it is extremely difficult to keep the upper arm and body relaxed while the fingers are making their efforts. This results in a lot of bad tension staying in the muscles and muscle memory, limiting and crippling progress, sometimes forever.

As we learn to make chord changes in this new way, without support, we must pay great attention to keeping the upper arm, upper body, and the rest of the body relaxed as much as we can (and we will always be able to do it more fully, every time we practice). As we support the Floating Arm completely with the larger muscles, and we are asking those muscles to do that in a relaxed way, we must make sure they remain relaxed during the effort we are making with our fingers, and this requires great attention during practice.

In addition to the ability to keep the larger muscles relaxed while the fingers are working, we also need to have made some progress with the "Foundation Exercises", especially the ones that develop the left hand fingers. "The Walking Exercises" from **"The Principles"**, done correctly and consistently, should be developing strength and stretch in your fingers. You need this development, as well as the first kind of development mentioned.

Making Chord Changes Without Support: Dive Bombing

I sometimes refer to making chord changes without support as "divebombing". In making this type of change, we would be picking up all the fingers from our last position, forming the shape of the chord in mid-air, (fully or partially) and then bringing the fingers down into position.

This more demanding way of making chord changes is often necessary and desirable, but it should be understood that making left hand changes *with* the use of support is an essential aspect of technique even at the highest levels of playing. In fact, without taking advantage of the leverage such movement gives, many extremely complicated passages, such as one finds in a Bach Lute Suite become uncomfortable, or impossible to execute at tempo.

So, you should realize that by learning to do left hand changes in the manner taught here, <u>with</u> support as well as <u>without</u>, you are also preparing yourself for guitaristic development at increasingly higher levels of technical demand.

Learning to Switch from G to D (With Support)
According to "The Principles of Correct Practice for Guitar"

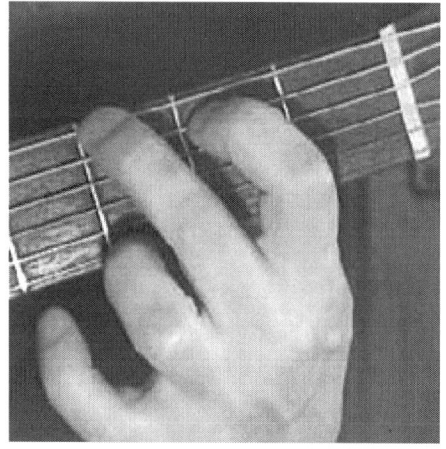

In the full G chord

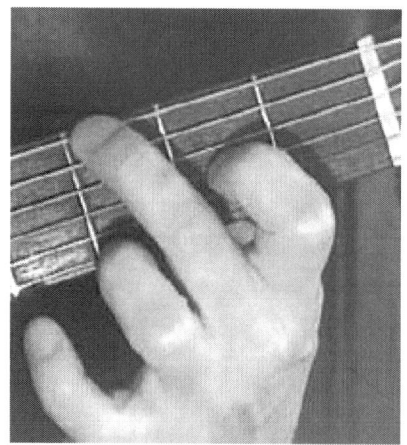

The 1st finger moves, the others remain

The GuitarPrinciples Path: Level One- Chords & Rhythm
Chords Five

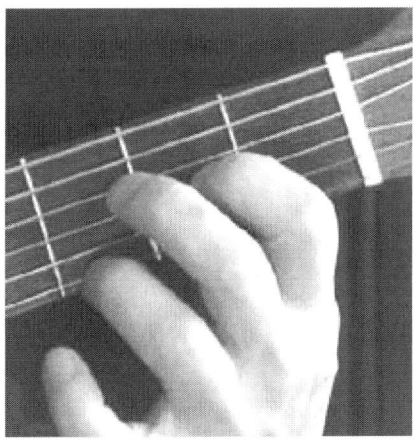

The 2nd finger begins to travel to the 1st string.

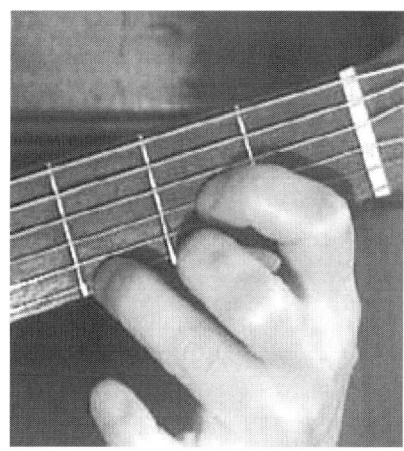

The 2nd finger places on the 1st string.

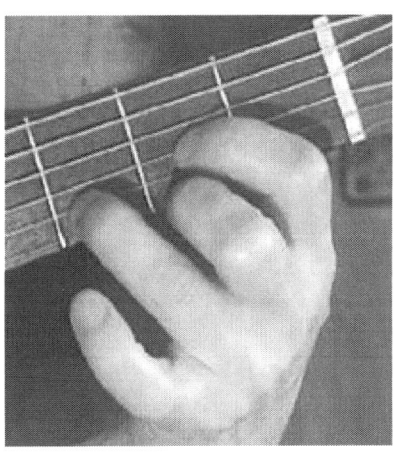

As you study these pictures, and try to make these moves as you see them done here, don't be surprised if it looks a lot easier in the pictures than it feels as you try them yourself! As your fingers develop in strength and flexibility, everything becomes easier (hopefully, you are doing the "Foundation Exercises" from "The Principles" to accomplish this).

The 3rd finger moves to the 2nd string.

The D chord is complete. Strum only the 4 top strings. Leave out the 5th and 6th string.

Study these pictures carefully, practice these moves according to the directions below:

With the fingers in the G major chord form, follow these steps to change to a D chord with support:

- Allow the 1st finger to become light, and drag it, (low to the strings, actually grazing them), over to the 3rd string, 2nd fret. Keep the heavy arm as you do so, and keep the whole body relaxed (especially shoulder) with "whole body awareness". DO IT AS SLOWLY AS NECESSARY TO MAINTAIN "WHOLE BODY RELAXATION, EVEN IF THAT MEANS TAKING 10 FULL SECONDS TO GET FROM ONE POSITION TO THE NEXT.

- Keeping the third finger where it is, bring the second finger all the way from the 6th string, 3rd fret to the 1st string, 2nd fret, behind the 3rd finger. Keep relaxing the shoulder and arm as you do this, because they will most likely tense. As you move the 2nd finger, move the elbow out slightly from the body; this helps to place the finger.

- From this position, check your fingers. Don't let them squeeze against one another, keep the space between them. Look at the fingertips, and make sure you are as close to the fret as you can get with each finger. Make sure the distal joint (tip joint) doesn't collapse.

- Finally, move the 3rd finger over to the 2nd string, 3rd fret, to complete the D chord. Play **each string, from the 4th to the 1st, to make sure it rings out clearly.** Check for any fingers leaning on an adjacent string and blocking the sound. This commonly happens with the 3rd finger bumping into the 1st string. Bend that joint! (but, relax!).

G to D With Less Support: Contrary Motion of 2 & 3 "In the Air"

After you are reasonably familiar and comfortable with doing this chord change as outlined above, try it with less support, relying more on the finger's developing ability to move independently of each other. Here, we will perform contrary motion with the 2nd & 3rd finger "in the air". (Details below)

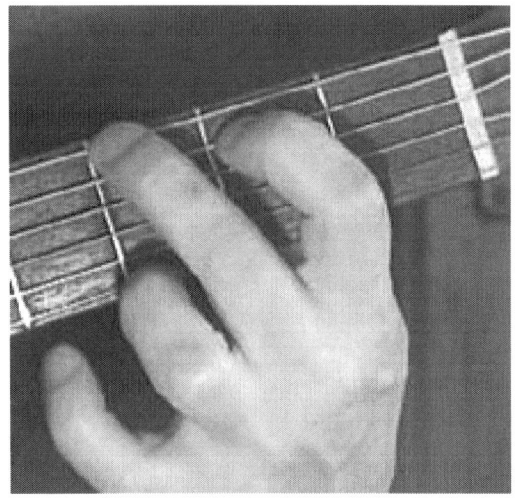 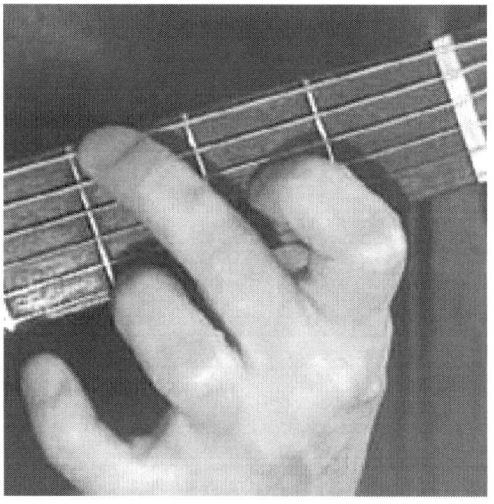

Begin as before with a full G   Bring the 1st over to 3rd string

The GuitarPrinciples Path: Level One - Chords & Rhythm
Chords Five

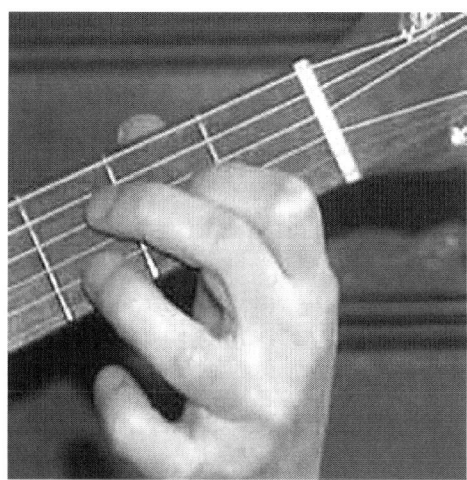

Release 2nd & 3rd from the G chord position, 3 is over its note.

Here is the crucial point where the 2nd finger must bend in while the 3rd finger remains extended. DO THIS SUPER SLOW AND SUPER RELAXED!

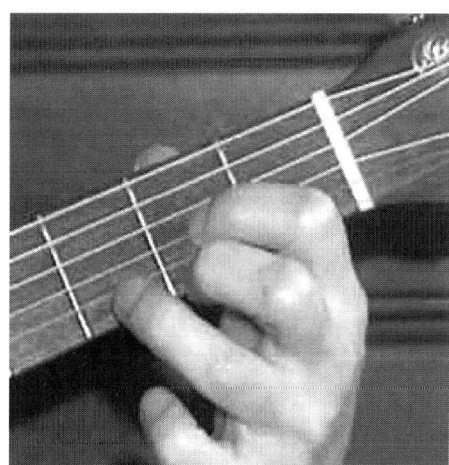

You must keep the space between the fingers. Here, the 2nd is bent while the 3rd stays extended. The 2nd finger must not be allowed to slide over the 2nd fret, it must stay behind it. If it keeps sliding over the fret, grab it with your right hand and move it back if you must. Eventually, as the fingers develop, it will stay put.

The ability to do contrary motion with two fingers that are next to each other is an extremely useful skill for guitar players. Understand that anyone can develop this ability if they go about it the right way. That means using "Posing", "No Tempo Practice", and "The Basic Practice Approach", as outlined in "The Principles".

Study the pictures showing how the hand looks when doing it wrong (pg.26). The 3rd finger tends to tense and squeeze against the 2nd finger, and this will very likely happen to you if you are a beginnner.

Changing G to D With Less Support

With the fingers in the G major chord form, follow these steps to change to a D chord with less support, performing contrary motion with the second and third fingers:

- Allow the 1st finger to become light, and drag it, (low to the strings, actually grazing them), over to the 3rd string, 2nd fret. Keep the heavy arm as you do so, and keep the whole body relaxed (especially shoulder) with "whole body awareness". DO IT AS SLOWLY AS YOU NEED TO DO IT TO MAKE SURE YOU MAINTAIN "WHOLE BODY RELAXATION", EVEN IF THAT MEANS TAKING 10 FULL SECONDS TO GET FROM ONE POSITION TO THE NEXT.

- Release pressure with the 2nd & 3rd fingers. Allow them to become light and float off the strings, in preparation for the contrary motion of the 2nd & 3rd fingers.

NOTE: The 2nd and 3rd finger, being next to each other, are greatly affected by each other's movements. When one fingers bends, the other tends to bend.

This is especially bad here, because if the 3rd finger bends WITH the 2nd finger as the 2nd finger is going for its note on the 1st string, <u>then</u> the 3rd finger will be moving away from where we need it! We need it to go on the 2nd string, <u>in front of</u> the 2nd finger, <u>NOT</u> alongside or behind it.

Because of this, we must train the 2nd and 3rd fingers to move in OPPOSITE directions at the same time. We must teach the 2nd finger to bend, or flex, toward the 1st string, WHILE the 3rd finger reaches, or extends, toward the 2nd string, 3rd fret.

Many players have the bad habit of allowing the 3rd to tense with the 2nd and move along with it over to the 1st string, and then after placing the 2nd finger, moving the 3rd finger toward its note on the 2nd string. This means having the 3rd finger move away from where it is going to end up, and then moving it back toward where it is going! This is double the work and double the time, and totally unacceptable. If your hand works this way, train this new habit into your fingers.

So, from the point that we left off above, do this:

While the arm weight is coming through the 1st finger, place your attention in both the 2nd and the 3rd fingers. Begin to move them simultaneously, bending the 2nd toward the 1st string, and extending the 3rd finger toward the 2nd string. Move the elbow out about two inches from the body to help the hand approach the neck at a better angle for placing the 2nd finger.

AT THE FIRST SIGN OF TENSION IN THE FINGERS, STOP, AND RELAX THE FINGERS, HAND, ARM AND WHOLE BODY. Rest assured that if the fingers are tensing (which they absolutely will if you are a beginner, or are undeveloped, or "wrongly developed"), then, your whole body is tensing, especially the shoulders. AND, you have probably stopped breathing!

If the fingers have begun to tense and squeeze against each other, STOP, relax them, and make another attempt. As you keep doing this over and over, you will develop the wonderful ability to move the two adjacent fingers in opposite directions at the same time. This ability will help you in many other chord changes as well.

Study the picture below, and pay great attention to the instructions about the joints being bent.

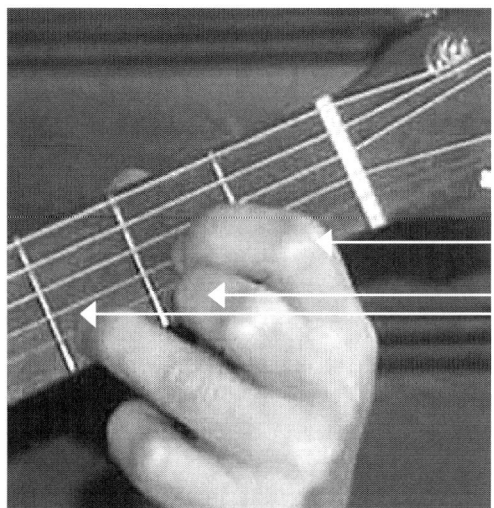

Keep a space here between hand & guitar neck.

This joint must be very bent. Don't' let it creep up to the fret and block the sound (see below).

This joint must be very bent also, so that it does not block the 1st string from ringing. Don't let this finger pull back too far from its fret and cause a buzz.

DOING IT WRONG!

Here are the things that normally go wrong……..

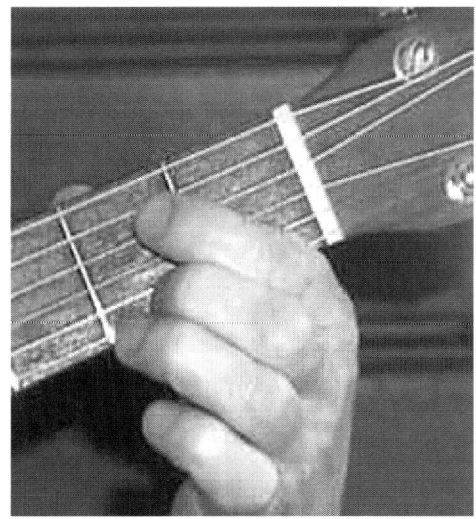

Instead of the 2nd & 3rd finger staying relaxed as they perform their contrary motion, they tense and stick together. Then, the whole arm tenses up.

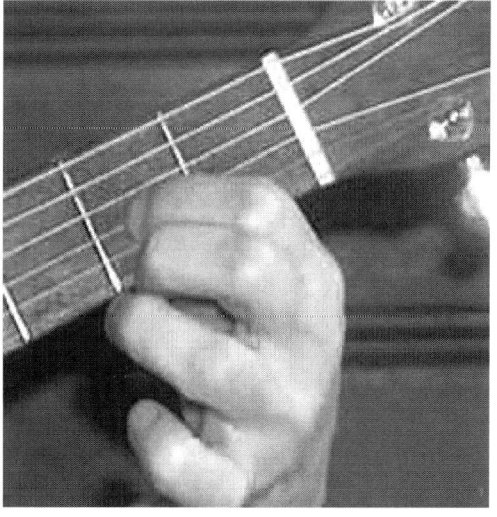

The 3rd finger travels with the 2nd, and ends up <u>away</u> from its note.

The GuitarPrinciples Path: Level One- Chords & Rhythm
Chords Five

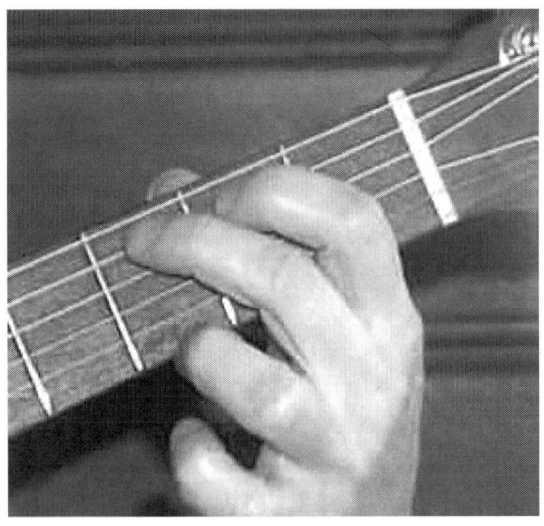

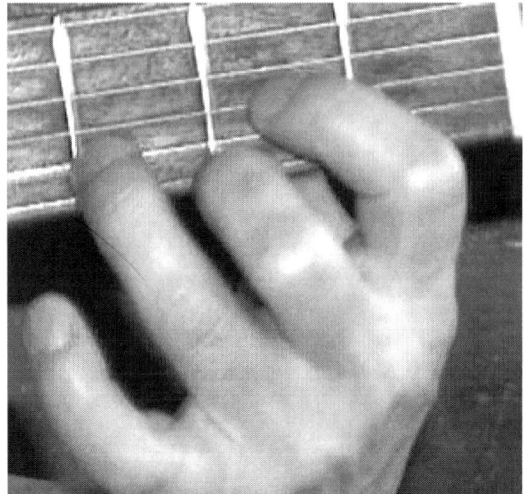

The hand does not stay out from the neck, but rather starts squeezing against the neck.

The 2nd finger cannot stay behind the 2nd fret, but keeps moving up against the fret, and so muffles the note. In this case, STOP and relax from the shoulder on down, make the fingers light, and slowly separate the 2nd and 3rd fingers, pulling the 2nd back and pushing the 3rd forward. You can even take your other hand and grab the fingers, and slowly pull them apart.

All fingers are too far from their frets. This will result in "buzzing" because the string will not be firmly against the fret. Or, it will result in extra effort to get the string to the fret.

Learning to Switch from D to A Minor (with support)

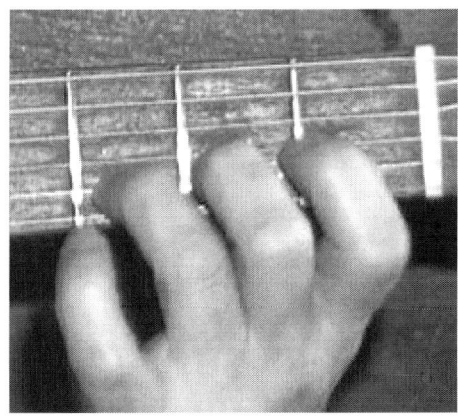

Release the 1st and 2nd fingers from the D chord, hold the 3rd for support.

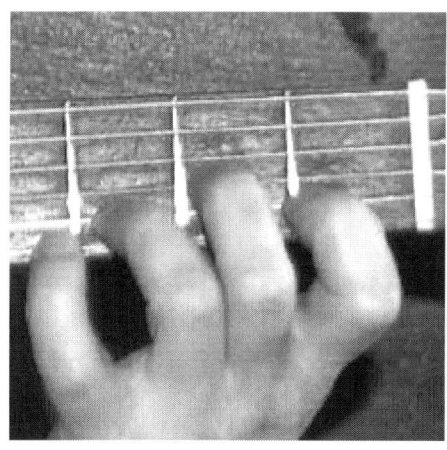

Place the 1st finger on the 2nd string, 1st fret, while still holding the 3rd finger in place.

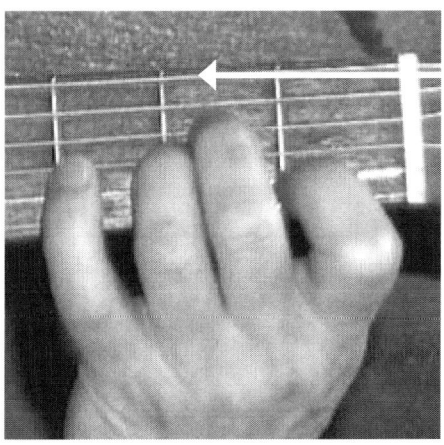

Completed A minor Chord

Shift weight to the 1st finger, release 3rd finger. Place "light" 2nd on 4th string, 2nd fret, and "light" 3rd finger on 3rd string, 2nd fret.

After they are in place, make the fingers firm, and relax the shoulder for "heavy arm".

- ❏ The 2nd & 3rd fingers "overlap" a bit, in order to get the 2nd as close to the fret as possible.

- ❏ Don't worry that it doesn't get as close as the 3rd. Just make sure there is no "buzz". Get a clear note. Strum only five strings. Leave out the 6th string.

- ❏ After you practice the D to Am with support, try it without support.

- ❏ Form the Am shape "in the air", doing contrary motion with the 2nd & 3rd before placing down.

The GuitarPrinciples Path: Level One- Chords & Rhythm
CHORDS FIVE

NOW, YOU'RE READY TO MAKE SOME MUSIC WITH THE SONG BELOW. ENJOY!

If you can do any fancier strums to this song, feel free to do so, but make sure that you can do a steady quarter note strum first, with singing. Remember, to strum all 6 strings for G, leave out the 6th string on Am, and leave out the 6th and 5th strings for the D chord. Practice the D to C change in the same manner as above for D to A minor.

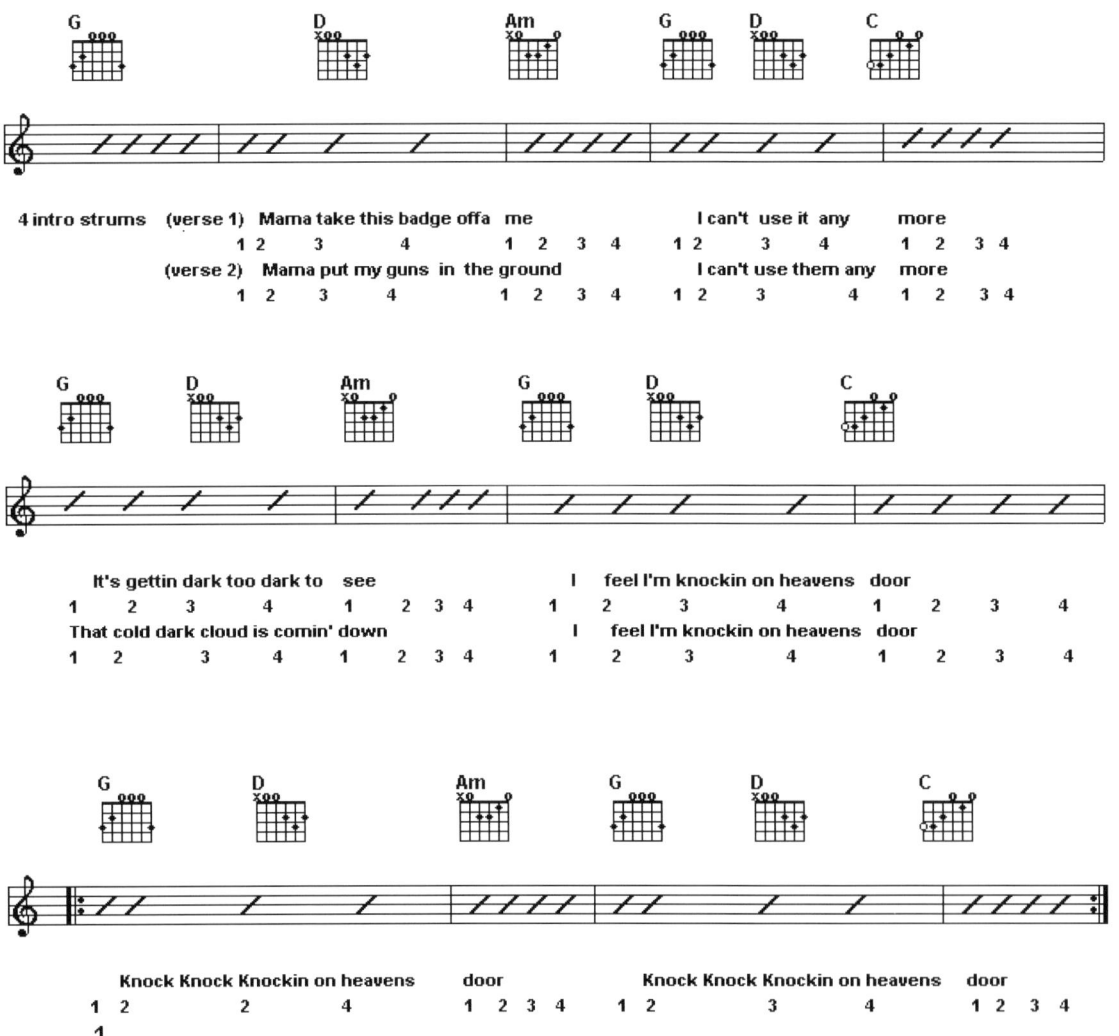

The GuitarPrinciples Path: Level One - Chords & Rhythm
Chords Five

Amazing Grace

31

THE GUITARPRINCIPLES PATH: RHYTHM ONE

The Purpose of this Course

There is no area of musical knowledge that is more misunderstood than rhythm. Many students start out very shaky in their grasp of the basic concepts, and remain shaky forever after. Many learn to copy rhythms by ear, and get by that way. But they never really grasp the system of rhythm notation itself, which makes it possible to function on a higher level as a musician.

The reason for this difficulty in grasping the fundamentals of rhythm is that rhythm, by nature, is abstract. It deals with the intangible dimension of time. The rudiments of rhythm, which must be grasped before the system of notation can really be worked with, are also abstract, and hard to "get a handle on" for many beginners. Then the whole situation is made worse by the fact that the usual guitar method book often distorts basic concepts, or leaves much too much unsaid (perhaps leaving it to the teacher to clarify, which often doesn't happen).

Because fundamental concepts are not adequately or clearly defined, the student cannot grasp more advanced concepts. As you will see, Lesson One begins with a clarification of the most basic concepts dealt with in music.

For now, in the beginning, <u>let us think of rhythm this way: a person who can play with "good rhythm" is a person who can make all the notes sound for exactly the right length of time in relation to each other, because he or she can make the right movements which will begin and end each sound at the exact right time.</u>

It is like a carpenter who can build a beautiful cabinet because he can measure all the wood to the right size, <u>and</u> has the skill to cut it to that size, not a millimeter bigger or smaller. When our music is "in rhythm" it has the right "shape". If the sounds are not measured out or "cut" correctly, the music will have a distorted shape to our mind's sense of time, as an improperly made cabinet would have a distorted shape to our eye's sense of form and line.

It must be understood that the person who can "copy" a rhythm by ear has a great natural ability, in fact, one that is more primary than the ability to read and write rhythms, just as being able to speak and understand words is more primary than the ability to read them. However, being able to read music opens up the possibility of endless growth in any style of music, as well as communication with other musicians.

This course is designed to foster these abilities:

1- The natural ability of the body and mind to perceive and perform rhythms. The mental understanding of the system of rhythm notation that has developed over hundreds of years, and is one half of what reading music is all about (the other, of course, being pitch).

The Definitions of the Basic Elements of Music: Notes & Beats

Before we can begin to understand rhythm, what it is, and how we work with it, we must understand a few basic definitions first. We must understand the definitions of the basic elements of music.

There are two words we hear often in our study of music, the word "note" and the word "beat". We hear somebody say "this note gets one beat; this note gets two beats". We might even hear "this note gets one half of a beat".

What is a note? A note is a sound, that's all. Sing La, any way you want, and you are singing a note. In fact, drummers call the sound they make when they hit the drum a note. You could slam the table and call that a note! So, a note is just a sound. As simple as this seems, it is important to be clear on it, because, like the word "beat", the word "note" is used to mean more than one thing. When you look at a piece of music, and see all the black and white ovals on the music paper, we say they are *notes*, but they are really *symbols* for notes, symbols for the sounds the musician makes, which are actually the notes.

What is a beat? This one is a little trickier. In fact, this one is so tricky; it is here that many people go wrong in understanding rhythm. When we hear music and tap our feet, we usually say, "I'm tapping the beat". That may be true in one sense of the word, but it is not true for musicians reading music. That is not what the beat is when it comes to learning to read music. If the tap of your foot were a beat, how could you divide the "tap" into two halves so that you could give a note a half beat?

No, a better word for that would be "pulse". When we tap our foot to the music, we are tapping the pulse of the music. Your heartbeat, for instance, thought of this way, would not be called a beat, but a pulse. This confusion in words that define "beat" is a big part of the problem.

So, what is a beat? A beat is a unit of time, measured by the foot going up and down.

Exercise 1: Creating Beats

Start tapping your foot slowly. Make sure your taps are steady with a smooth motion of the foot, having the same amount of time in between each one, as in one tap every second. Start counting 1 2 3 4 as you tap, over and over. The TIME in between your taps is one beat.

Time is always measured by something moving. The second hand on a clock moves in a circle, and when it does one round, we call it a minute. We divide that circle into sixty parts and when the second hand travels from one part to the next, we say ONE SECOND has gone by.

So, a beat is an amount of time measured by your moving foot. If you use a metronome to measure the beat, then the beat is the time in between metronome clicks, not the click itself.

Definition of Tempo

Minutes and seconds are always the same. On every clock, minutes and seconds are the same, but beats are not always the same. If you tap your foot slowly, the beat is long. If you tap your foot fast, the beat is short. So, how fast your foot goes determines how long or short the beat is. When we say, "a fast beat" we really mean a fast pulse, a fast tap of the foot. Technically speaking, the beat is not fast; IT IS SHORT, a short amount of time. If our foot is tapping slowly, there is a longer time between taps, and we say, "the beat is slow", really, the beat is now longer.

So we will understand that the common way of speaking is to use phrases like "the beat is slow" or "the beat is fast", but really, the true meaning is "the beat is long", or "the beat is short". Later on, with more advanced things, understanding beats and rhythm in this way is important. That is why I mention it here. But we will agree that saying "the beat is slow" is the same thing as saying, "the beat is long", likewise, saying "the beat is fast" is the same as saying "the beat is short".

Having understood that, we will introduce another important word for understanding rhythm, the word "tempo". Tempo means the speed of the pulse; how fast the tap of your foot is. Fast tempos give us fast pulses and short beats; slow tempos give us slow pulses and long beats.

Measuring out Time to Sound: Why a Musician is Like a Carpenter

So, we have already learned how to measure out beats by tapping our foot and counting. Let's try measuring out some sounds with different lengths. When a carpenter builds something, he works with two things: the material of wood, and the dimension of space. He has to take his wood and cut it into pieces of just the right length, and then fit them all together. If he is the tiniest bit off in measuring and cutting one of his pieces, his finished product will be all lopsided (like every piece of woodwork I ever tried to make!). So, measuring his material, wood, precisely in terms of the dimension of space, is crucial to the finished product.

For musicians, our material is sound, and our dimension is time. We must measure out the exact right amount of time for each sound we make. And just as the carpenter has his units of measurement, namely inches and feet, we have the beat as our measuring unit. We must give the right number of beats, or sometimes a part of a beat (maybe a half-beat or even a quarter beat) to every sound we make. If we are off in our measuring of time to the sounds we make, our music will be as lopsided as my carpentry projects were!

So, we have already learned how to measure out beats by tapping our foot and counting. Let's try measuring out some sounds with different lengths of beats.

Exercise 2: Singing One Note Per Beat

Count   1   2   3   4

Foot   ↓   ↓   ↓   ↓

1- Tap your foot to a steady beat, and count 1 2 3 4 every time your foot hits the floor.

2- Now, keep your foot tapping, but instead of counting, sing LA LA LA LA every time your foot goes down.

You are now singing notes that are each receiving one beat.

Exercise 3: Strumming One Chord Per Beat

1- **Tap** your foot to a steady beat, and **count** 1 2 3 4 every time your foot hits the floor.

2- Now, keep your foot tapping, but instead of counting, **sing LA LA LA** LA every time your foot goes down.

3- Take your guitar and **strum** a chord every time your foot hits the floor.

NOTE: You can use the very simple easy G chord, the first shown below, or one of the others) Refer to the "Beginner Path Chord Lessons" for more details. Or, you can even strum the strings "open", meaning with no fingers down on the frets.

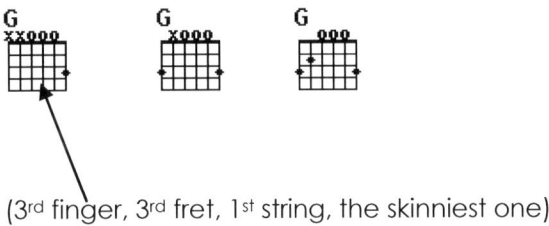

(3rd finger, 3rd fret, 1st string, the skinniest one)

Also, refer to "The Principles of Correct Practice For Guitar" for exact instructions on holding and using the pick.

Notice something very obvious and very important: when your hand is strumming, it is doing a down motion, during which it strikes the strings to make the sound. It is then doing an up motion, but is missing the strings on its way up, because we don't want to strike the strings on the way up. <u>This symbol, **(↑)** is an up arrow in parenthesis, and means don't strike the strings on the way up.</u>

Count   1   2   3   4

Hand   ↓ (↑) ↓ (↑) ↓ (↑) ↓ (↑)

We want to strike the strings to make a new sound a total of four times, once every time the foot hits the floor. If the pick were to strike the strings on the way up as well as the way down, it would strike the strings a total of eight times, which we don't want, at least not now.

This may seem obvious, but later on, it will be important to understand this, because as rhythms get more complicated, guitar students very often STOP the motion of the hand in mid air, and re-start again. This is very bad, and will cause distorted rhythm. **The hand and arm must keep a continuous motion during strumming.**

When doing strums that have a lot of space between them, such as a whole note, we may stop the hand, but most often this is not the case. An advanced player may be able to do this, but you should keep to the rule of maintaining the up and down motion of the hand following the foot, even during long spaces in the strumming. This will keep you out of trouble.

So, pay attention to the hand motion going up, even though you are not striking the strings with this motion. Later, you will strike the strings with this motion, sometimes during every up strum, and sometimes only on some of the up strums. Paying attention now will give you control later on.

Exercise 4: Increasing Awareness of The Up Motion Of The Hand

On this next exercise, tap, and strum as in Ex. 3, but this time, instead of counting, say "down" when your hand and foot go down, and "up" when they go up.

Make sure the foot movement follows the hand movement. The hand goes down as the foot goes down, and the hand goes up as the foot goes up.

Count	1		2		3		4	
Hand	↓	(↑)	↓	(↑)	↓	(↑)	↓	(↑)
Say	down	up	down	up	down	up	down	up

Exercise 5: Singing & Playing Long Notes

We have just sung and played notes that get one beat. Now we will sing notes that get two beats. As in written music, we will divide the beats by placing a horizontal line in between every group of 4 beats.

1- **Tap** your foot to a steady beat, **and count 1 2 3 4** every time your foot hits the floor.

2- As your foot taps, **sing LA**, making it last for beat one and two. You will sing one long LA for both beats, then say 3, 4.

Sing:	LA	-	A	3	4	|	LA	-	A	3	4
Tap:	1		2	3	4	|	1		2	3	4

You are now singing longer notes, notes that get TWO BEATS.

3- Now, **tap** your foot, **count** out loud, and **play** when you say 1 and when you say 3. Even though the hand only plays the strings on 1 & 3, keep it moving up and down for the other beats, just don't hit the strings.

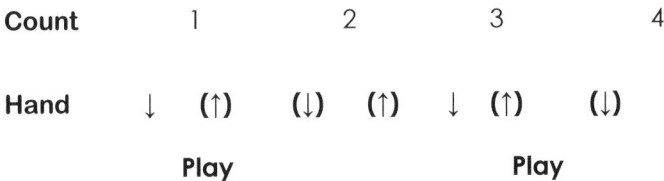

You are now playing chords that last two beats each.

Exercise 6: Mixing Notes of Different Lengths

The ability to tap the foot and sing (and play) sounds of different lengths is essential to becoming a musician. It should begin at the very beginning of music instruction, but often does not.

1- **Tap** your foot to a steady beat, **and count 1 2 3 4** every time your foot hits the floor.

2- **Sing LA** for the number of beats indicated (you begin a new note with each bold LA):

Length of Note:	___|___ | _____|_|_____|_|_____
Sing:	**LA**-A-**LA**-A | **LA**-A-A-**LA** |**LA**-A-A-A | **LA**-**LA**-A-A |
Tap:	1 2 3 4 1 2 3 4 1 2 3 4 1 2 3 4

3- After you are comfortable with singing LA for Exercise 6, try playing a chord instead of singing LA.

Understand that you will have to do this over and over many times. Expect to get mixed up and confused as you do the exercise. Stop, re-think what you are doing, collect yourself, and make another attempt. It will get easier and easier.

Lesson Review: Key Definitions

Note- a sound. The written symbols for notes we see on music are referred to as "notes", but they are symbols for notes. Notes are sounds.

Beat- a unit of time, measured by the foot going up and down. The tap of the foot is sometimes called the beat, but it is really the "pulse".

Pulse- the "tap" of the foot, marking the beat. Also, the "feeling" of the beat, as we feel the "pulse" or beat of our heart. The "tap" of the foot is really how we measure the beginning and the end of the unit of time we call the beat.

Tempo- the speed of the beat. technically, the speed of the pulse of the music. When the pulse is fast, beats are short. When the pulse is slow, beats are long.

Strumming- We keep a continuous up and down motion of the hand when strumming, whether or not we are striking the strings on each down and up motion.

THE GUITARPRINCIPLES PATH: RHYTHM TWO

Dividing the Beat: Using Counting Symbols

Now that we understand that a beat is an amount of time measured by the foot going up and down, let's look a little further into the concept.

Because we are going to be working with this unit of measurement, we need to be able to do a few things with it. We need to group beats together, so we can give some sounds a long amount of time. It's the same as if we were using inches to measure something. Sometimes we would have to group inches together to measure long things. Something maybe five inches long, for instance. Some things may be shorter than an inch, so we need to divide the inch into smaller parts.

The Parts of the Beat

We do this with beats, also. We divide them in half and sometimes in quarters (which makes for short notes) and because of that, we have to know the different "parts", or really "places" in the beat.

Beginning of the Beat

The beat begins at the point in time when your foot is DOWN and is just about to start its round trip up and back.

Middle of the Beat

The middle of the beat is where and when the foot is UP.

End of the Beat

The beat ends when the foot comes back down again. <u>The end of one beat is simultaneously the beginning of the next beat.</u>

The Use of Counting Symbols

In order to make our notes sound for the correct amount of time, we must not only understand the parts of the beat, such as the beginning, middle and end, we must also have a way of knowing WHERE we are in the beat at any given moment in playing. We must KNOW where, and when the beginning of the beat is. We must KNOW where, and when the middle of the beat is. We must know this because we are going to have to **PLAY** certain notes **EXACTLY** on the beginning, or middle of certain beats.

The way we know where we are in the beat is through the use of counting symbols. For instance, when you tapped your foot and counted along with it, you were using a counting symbol. Numbers, 1, 2, 3, 4, are the counting symbols used for the beginning of beats. When the foot goes down, and you say a number, you know you are at the beginning of the beat. The beginning of the beat is also called the **Downbeat**.

Counting Symbols are signposts that are written under parts of the beat, to tell us where we are in the beat; beginning, middle, or some smaller division. You must be able to write them in, and to say them in correct time while tapping the foot. If you can't do this, you don't understand the rhythm. You will be required to write in the counting symbols under the notes later on. Experienced musicians don't need to write in the counting symbols, unless they are uncomfortable with a rhythm, and need to clarify it for themselves. You, as the student, will need to do this to learn rhythm notation, and to test your understanding.

The middle of the beat is a little more difficult to discern, since it is not as strongly marked as the downbeat, which is easy to tell since the foot is down. To tell when we are at the middle of the beat (the foot is up), we use the counting symbol and, usually written with **a plus sign (+), such as 1 + 2 + 3 + 4 +.**

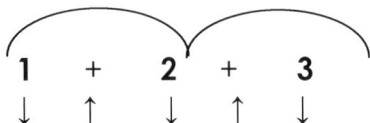

The illustration above shows the path of the foot traveling up and down as it measures out the beat. The counting symbol **1** marks the beginning of the first beat. The + marks the middle of the beat, when the foot is up, **2** marks the end of the first beat and the beginning of the second beat, etc.

So, the middle of the beat is where and when your foot is UP, and that divides the beat in half. This is also called the **Upbeat.**

Counting symbols are the tools we use to make sure we are dividing time up correctly when we play. If you cannot write in the counting symbols under the notes of music you are playing, then you DO NOT understand the rhythm. In order to write in the counting symbols under the notes, you must be able to **answer three questions for every note :**

1- **How many beats does this note get?**

2- **Which beats does it get?**

3- **What counting symbol is used to represent that beat or part of a beat?** (e.g. "+" is used to represent the second half of the second beat).

For example, we may say: "This note gets two beats, and they are the first and second beats in the measure. The counting symbols marking those beats are **1** and **2**."

Rhythm is the relationship in time that sounds have to one another. To do the right rhythm is to make the notes have the correct relationship of time to one another, which means they must sound for the exact length of time they are supposed to. If a sound is supposed to be one beat long, it must BE one beat long. If it is supposed to be one half of a beat, it must BE one half of a beat. (One of the implications of this for the player is to understand that control over the exact beginning and ending of each note is of primary importance**)**.

The anchor of your measurement of the beat is, of course, your steadily tapping foot.

Exercise 1: Dividing the Beat in Half

1- Start tapping your foot to a steady beat.

2- When your foot goes down, **say down**. When it is up, **say up**.

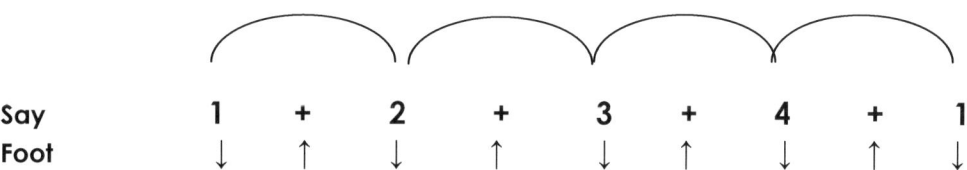

3- After this is going smooth and steady, use counting symbols instead of DOWN and UP. So now, say **1 + 2 + 3 + 4 +,** over and over as you **tap** your foot.

You are now dividing the beat in half. Every time you say "and"(+) you are marking the middle of the beat, where your foot is up.

Exercise 2: Singing notes that get ½ beat.

Repeat Exercise 1, and after saying **1 + 2 + 3 + 4 +** over and over a few times, replace each Counting Symbol with a sung **LA**.

The GuitarPrinciples Path: Level One - Chords & Rhythm
Rhythm Two

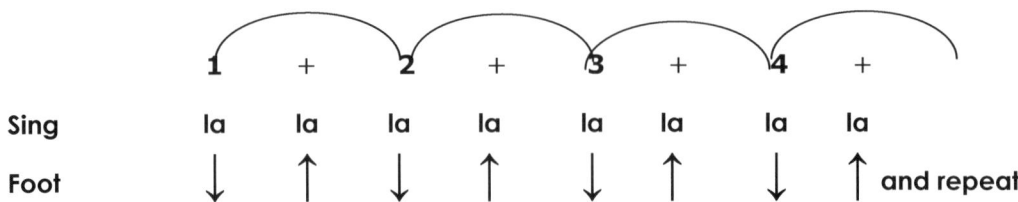

You are now singing notes that get one half of a beat. This is done often in playing, and is mixed in with notes of other lengths to create interesting rhythms. If you take your guitar and strum a chord for each LA, do this strum with a DOWN motion of the pick or thumb as the foot goes down, followed by an UP strum when the foot comes up.

Exercise 3: Mixing Notes of Different Lengths, Including Half Beats

   1- **Count** and **tap** foot: 1 2 3 4 | 1+2+3+4+ | 1 2 3 4 | 1+2+3+4+

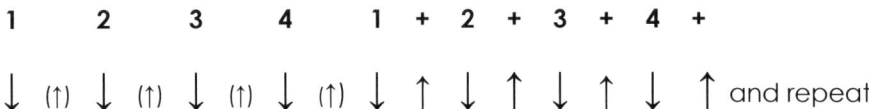

   2- Sing **LA** instead of saying counting symbols. So, instead of "1+2+", **say "LA LA LA LA"** to the same rhythm, as your foot taps.

   3- **Strum** your guitar to this rhythm (use open strings if you don't know any chords yet). Use a down strum when the foot goes down, and an up strum when the foot goes up.

The arrows in parenthesis indicate your foot going up, but no counting symbol is used or spoken.

When counting rhythms:

- We will **always** say the numbers to indicate downbeats.

- We may or may not use the other counting symbols (+, etc.) depending on whether there are notes being played on those parts of the beat.

- Whether there are notes being played, or silent time being counted out (see "Rests", Lesson Six), **the foot will always be in motion, up and down.**

Here are two more rhythms to practice. These rhythms are common strumming patterns for guitar:

Exercise 4

1   2 3+4+ | 1 2 3+4+

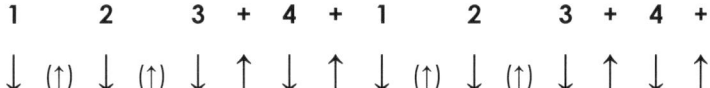

Remember, the pick only strikes the strings on the arrows NOT in parenthesis. Just keep it moving for the arrows in parenthesis.

Exercise 5:

1 2+3 4+ | 1 2+ 3 4+ |

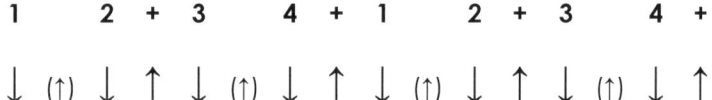

Lesson 2 Review: Key Definitions

Downbeat: beginning of the beat, when the foot is down.

Upbeat: middle of the beat, when the foot is up.

Counting Symbols: are signposts that are written under parts of the beat, to tell us where we are in the beat: beginning, middle, or some smaller division.

Rhythm: means the relationship in time that sounds have to one another. To do the right rhythm is to make the notes have the correct relationship of time to one another.

If you can't write in the counting symbols under notes, you do not understand the rhythm. You must answer <u>3 questions for each note</u>:

1. How many beats (or part of a beat) does the note get?
2. Which beats does it get?
3. What counting symbols are used to mark those beats or parts of beats?

THE GUITARPRINCIPLES PATH: RHYTHM THREE

The Proportionate Relationship of Note Values

We are going to begin to learn the fundamentals of the system of rhythm notation that has developed over the centuries. This system enables musicians to precisely write down a rhythm so that other musicians can duplicate it. Just as we write down words to precisely communicate thoughts to other people, we can set down HOW MUCH TIME we want someone to give to the sounds they make when playing.

In order to do this, we had to have some standard of measuring the time, and we have already seen that it is the BEAT. We have learned that the beat is the standard unit of time, and it is measured by the foot going up and down.

Why Is Rhythm Important?

Before we go further, I want to make sure you understand WHY it is important that we give each sound we make its proper amount of time. Do this: tap your foot to a steady beat and sing "Happy Birthday". (Go ahead, DO it!)

Notice a couple of things. When you start, the word "Happy", it gets all crammed into the first beat, that is, you say it kind of fast, fitting it into the time it takes for your foot to make its first trip up and down. Then, on "Birthday" each syllable gets its own beat. "Birth" starts on a downbeat, and "day" starts the next time your foot goes down. The word "you" is longer. It gets two trips of your foot, or two beats.

Now, realize this basic fact. If you changed these relationships around, if you gave, for instance, the first word "Happy" two beats for each of its syllables, and then "Birth" and "day" were crammed into one beat, and "to" and "you" each got, say, four beats, well then, it sure wouldn't sound like "Happy Birthday"!

What is the point? The point is that without the proper time relationships, THERE IS NO HAPPY BIRTHDAY! There may be something else, but it ain't Happy Birthday! If I am the person that wrote the song, I must have a way of making sure you do what I intend, I have to make sure you give all the notes their proper time value, and that they are all in the correct relationship to one another.

Note Values

So, how do I tell somebody "make a sound, and hold it for two beats, then make another sound, and make it last one beat, then make a sound for a half a beat, etc"? Well, here is where we will get into some concepts that are USUALLY the starting point for a student's introduction to rhythm. I am going to lay out these concepts, AND I am going to include all the vital understandings that should go along with them.

Below, you see what are commonly called "notes". This is what we see when we look at music. Of course, we know they are not notes, because notes are sounds. These are SYMBOLS for notes, and they carry a MEANING along with them, and the meaning is made evident in their names.

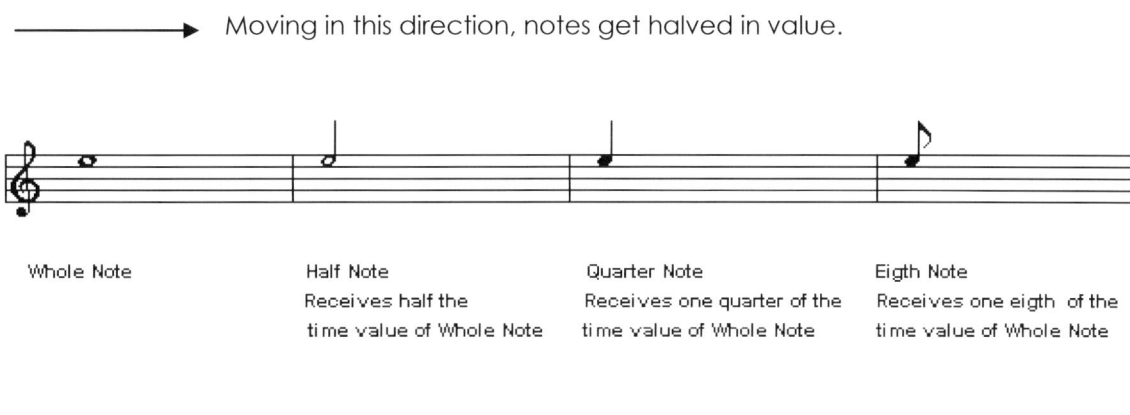

Why is that funny little football called a WHOLE NOTE? Well, because it gets a "whole" lot of time. That's a joke, (not very funny, I know). The point is this: I don't know how much time it is going to get. The note symbols you see above get different amounts of time in different pieces of music depending on a thing called the **Time Signature**, which we will learn about later. The time signature will give us more information that will determine how much time each note symbol gets. But I do know this: whatever amount of time the whole note gets, the HALF NOTE will get half of that time. That is why it is called a half note.

The next one, the QUARTER NOTE, is called a quarter note because it gets one quarter (one fourth) the time of the whole note. The EIGHTH NOTE gets one eighth of the time of the whole note.

So, if we move from whole note, to half, to quarter, to eighth, the notes are halved in value, each one worth one half of the one before it. If we move from eighth note to quarter, to half, to whole note, the notes double in value, each one worth twice what the one before it was worth.

Notice, all the note values get their names from their relationships to the WHOLE note. This brings up an understanding that is vital to grasping the entire system of rhythm notation, and one that is dreadfully lacking for so many students.

The note values, whole, half, quarter and eighth notes, HAVE NO ABSOLUTE VALUE. They only have a relative value. They are in a **PROPORTIONATE RELATIONSHIP TO ONE ANOTHER.**

In other words, when that good ole' method book your teacher started you on tells you "hello budding guitar player, this is a quarter note, it gets one beat", they are LYING to you. True, it's a white lie; they have good intentions. They figure you are not going to understand the real story, so they try to simplify it for you. The problem is, they never bother to explain the real story to you later on!

It's like when you were three years old and your mother told you never to cross the street unless someone was holding your hand. What if no one ever told you differently as you got older, no one ever updated your belief system. That is a useful and workable attitude when you are three, but hey, you're gonna look a little funny when you're twenty-five and still asking people to walk you across the street!

If you were three years old, I'd tell you the quarter note gets one beat, but if you were three years old, you probably wouldn't be reading this. So, now you know the real deal.

To summarize:

The whole note is worth 2 times the half
The half note is worth 1/2 of the whole.

The half note is worth 2 times the quarter
The quarter note is worth 1/2 the half

The quarter note is worth 2 times the eighth
The eighth note is worth 1/2 the quarter

What is a Proportionate Relationship?

In case you are not clear on exactly what a proportionate relationship is, let me explain it very simply.

Imagine you are going to a job interview with three of your friends. The boss sees you are obviously more intelligent than your friends, so he says "look, I'll pay you the most money, and your friend John, well, I'll pay him HALF of what I pay you. And your friend Steve, he's not too bright, I'm only going to pay him a QUARTER of what I pay you. And that guy Joe, he's a real dummy, he's only going to get an EIGHTH of what I pay you." I think you get the point. Nobody knows HOW MUCH they are making; that would be an ABSOLUTE VALUE. They only know how much they are making in RELATION to each other. That is a RELATIVE VALUE.

All you know, being the smartest guy there, is that you are going to make a WHOLE lot of money, at least more than your friends! Now, your friends are REAL interested in how much you are going to get! They ask you, but all you can say is "I don't know. The boss said he will post on the bulletin board every Friday how much I am making". So next Friday, everyone crowds around the bulletin board, and sees you are making $10 an hour. So, now John knows he is getting $5 an hour, Steve knows he's getting $2.50, and poor old Joe is going home with a buck and a quarter for every hour of his sweat!

The good news is that next week business is better, so you find out you are making $14 an hour, and, of course, everyone else is happy for your good fortune! Now, John is making $7.00 and hour, Steve is making $3.50, and old Joe is quite proud of his $1.75!

The Time Signature

Understanding the time signature is usually the beginning of the end for most students' understanding of rhythm. This is because of the time that you are told what it is, (usually at the beginning of learning to read notes) it is not possible for you to actually understand what you are told.

The **time signature** is the two numbers you see at the beginning of a piece of music. The two numbers are stacked one on top of the other. They each tell you something.

Here are some examples of common time signatures you will see in music.

Examples of most common time signatures

The Bottom Number of the Time Signature

Let's find out what the bottom number means.

<u>Pay attention now:</u> the bottom number of the time signature tells you what kind of note (whole, half, quarter or eighth) gets one beat.

WHY is it important that the bottom number tells you what kind of note gets one beat?

Because the bottom number is like the BULLETIN BOARD. It gives an amount, or a value, to one of the notes, so now all the values of the other notes (that you don't know) can be figured out by using the value that you do know. So, if there is a **2** on the bottom, it means the half note gets **one** beat (2 on the bottom always stands for half note).

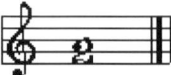

If the half note gets one beat, then I know these things:

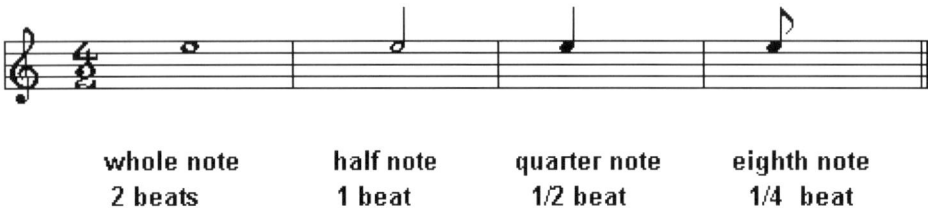

whole note	half note	quarter note	eighth note
2 beats	1 beat	1/2 beat	1/4 beat

- The half note gets one beat, because the time signature tells me that.

- The whole note gets two beats, because it always gets double what the half note gets.

- The quarter note gets ½ beat, because it always gets one half of what the half note gets.

- The eighth note gets ¼ of a beat, since it gets one half of what the quarter note gets.

Now, one other thing about the half note getting one beat: you will probably never see it! This Time signature is rarely used, except for ancient music. If you play the classical guitar, you may very well see it. However, the important thing for our purposes here is to understand the logic of how time signatures work.

Now, we will look at a time signature that you will see, in fact, all the time.

The Quarter Note Gets One Beat

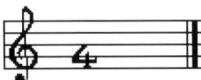

What you will see most often is the quarter note getting one beat. If there is a 4 on the bottom of the time signature, it is telling you the quarter note gets one beat (4 stands for quarter). In this case, the value of the other notes is arranged as follows:

The GuitarPrinciples Path: Level One- Chords & Rhythm
Rhythm Three

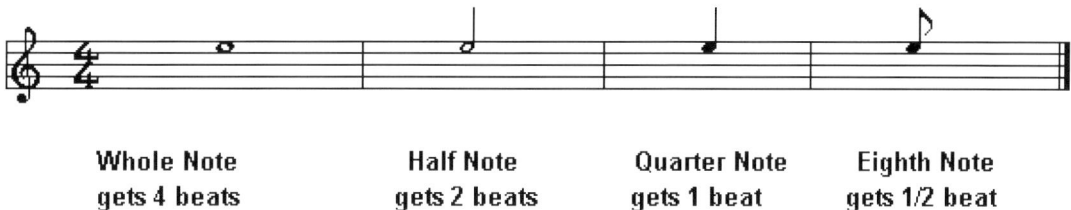

| Whole Note | Half Note | Quarter Note | Eighth Note |
| gets 4 beats | gets 2 beats | gets 1 beat | gets 1/2 beat |

- The quarter note gets one beat, because the bottom number of the time signature tells me that.

- The whole note gets four beats, because it always gets double what the half note gets.

- The half note gets two beats, because it always gets double what the quarter note gets.

- The eighth note gets ½ of a beat, because it always gets one half of what the quarter note gets.

This is the most common situation you will encounter: the quarter note getting one beat. In fact, the time signature 4/4, is called "common time".

The Eighth Note Gets One Beat

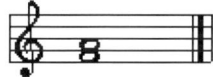

Now, we have the eighth note getting one beat. You will see this often. It is common that students who are learning to read music will have spent quite a while treating quarter notes as getting one beat. In fact, even being told "quarter notes get one beat", instead of being told "quarter notes *sometimes* get one beat". Then, they have trouble dealing with the situation where an eighth note gets one beat.

When the eighth note gets one beat, we have this situation:

| Whole Note | Half Note | Quarter Note | Eighth Note |
| gets 8 beats | gets 4 beats | gets 2 beat | gets 1 beat |

- ❏ The eighth note gets one beat, because the bottom number of the time signature tells me that.

- ❏ The quarter note gets two beats, because it always gets double what the eighth note gets.

- ❏ The half note gets four beats, because it always gets double what the quarter note gets.

- ❏ The whole note gets eight beats, because it always gets double what the half note gets.

The Top Number of the Time Signature

New Terms:

Measure: A section of music containing the number of beats indicated by the top number of the time signature. Measures are marked off by bar lines.

Bar Line: A vertical line used to section off the music staff into measures.

The top number of the time signature tells you how many beats are allowed in each measure. If you are writing music, you must make sure that each measure contains the proper number of beats, no more and no less. So, we count up the value of the notes in each measure to see if they add up to the correct amount.

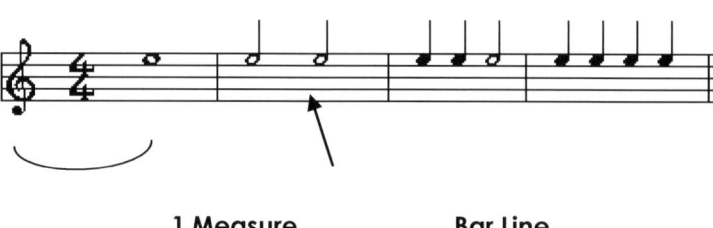

1 Measure   Bar Line

The top number tells me that there are four beats allowed in each measure. All of the above combinations equal four beats. Of course, understanding that the bottom number gives the quarter note one beat is essential to figuring out the notes that are allowed on top.

 **WRONG**

These measures are **not** allowed because they have five beats instead of four.

Here there are three beats allowed in each measure, and the eighth note gets one beat, and the quarter gets two. So, any of the above combinations are allowed.

 **WRONG**

These measures are wrong; they have too many beats. Notice, a half note or whole note cannot be used here. Since the eighth note gets one beat, the half note would get four, and only three beats are allowed in each measure.

Incomplete Measures

Very often a song or piece of music will not begin on beat number one. So, the first measure will appear to have fewer beats than it should have. In measure one below, you see three quarter notes in 4/4 time. We must count the first one as beat 2, followed by 3 and 4. In the second measure, we start on beat 3. You figure out the last measure!

When you have this situation, merely start counting on 1, and begin playing on the count that coincides with the first note.

    2 3 4   3 4   4

Lesson Review: Key Understandings

Note Values: The Note Values: whole, half, quarter, and eighth notes, tell us how much time to give to each note. They have no ABSOLUTE VALUE, but only a RELATIVE TIME VALUE. They are in a **Proportionate Relationship** to each other.

Time Signature: Two numbers, in fraction form, appearing at the beginning of a piece of music. The bottom number tells us WHICH OF THE NOTE VALUES GETS ONE BEAT, so we can figure out how much time the others get by using the **Proportionate Relationship** that exists between them.

The top number tells us how many beats are allowed in each measure.

THE GUITARPRINCIPLES PATH : RHYTHM FOUR

Strumming Rhythms Written in Music Notation

At this point, we have had some experience in strumming chords to different rhythms, and singing notes to different rhythms, as we looked at diagrams representing those rhythms. Then, we learned a lot about note symbols, what they mean and how they are written.

Now, we are going to put all of this together. We are going to strum rhythms that are notated in conventional music notation. Depending on your level as a guitarist, you can do anything from using open strings to strum, (no fingers placed on frets) to using one of the easy chords below.

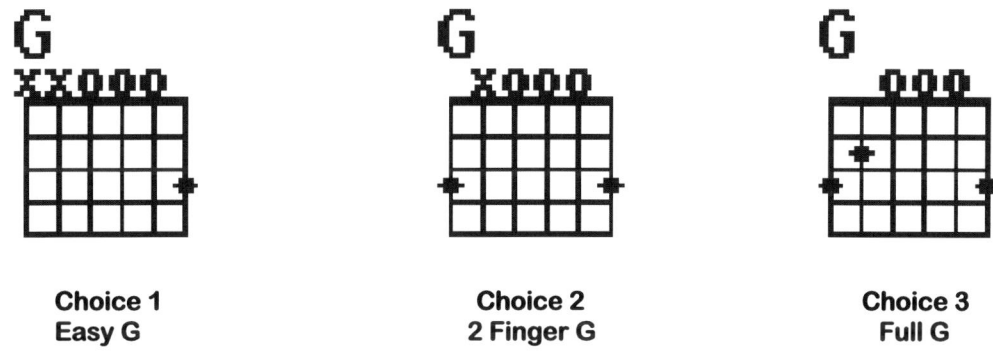

Choice 1
Easy G

Choice 2
2 Finger G

Choice 3
Full G

Use whichever chord you are comfortable with. (The one finger G chord, Choice 1, is for beginners). If you use Choice 2, block the string marked "x" with the side of the finger. For Choice 3, don't include x'd out strings in your strum. We are not changing chords here, which allows the focus to be only on the rhythmic aspect of playing. If you can easily change chords, then you can use different chords to make it more interesting, as long as you do the rhythm exactly. (Note: If you are learning the other chords in the "Changing Chords" section, use those, of course).

Realize that the note symbols in these rhythm exercises do not represent individual pitches, as they usually do in reading music. They represent only the LENGTH OF TIME the sound of the chord lasts.

Also, notice we are in 4/4 time, so the quarter note gets one beat, the half note gets two, and the whole note gets four beats.

Instructions: Place and hold chord. Tap your foot to a steady beat. Strum where required by the music. **Count** out loud as you do so. THESE INSTRUCTIONS MUST BE FOLLOWED EXACTLY, OR YOU WILL NOT DEVELOP THE NECESSARY SKILLS TO DEVELOP FURTHER!

Begin to tap your foot and count out four beats to "set the beat" in your mind and body. Continue tapping and counting while playing.

IMPORTANT: The saying of the counting symbols to the tapping foot is supposed to sound just like the rhythm written in notes. For this reason, in a rhythm like the one in Exercise 1 below, say the beat that the note begins on LOUDER than the beats for which the note is merely ringing. You can do this simply by whispering the 2, 3, 4. This will give a better approximation of the rhythm.

Say   1 2 3 4 | 1 2 3 4, etc.

Exercise 1: Strumming Whole Notes

1. **Tap** foot, **count** out loud, saying counting symbols. **Whisper** 2, 3, 4.

2. **Tap** foot, **sing LA** for each note. So, each measure has one long LA, each lasting four beats.

3. **Tap** foot, **count** out loud, **strum** a chord on beat 1. Let it ring for beats 2, 3, and 4.

IMPORTANT: Always keep the hand in motion when strumming. In this exercise, you only need to strike the strings once per measure, but still move the hand up and down for beats 2, 3 and 4. This will be important later on.

ALSO IMPORTANT: SET your beat before you begin by counting and tapping 1,2,3,4, BEFORE beginning.

Things to Be Clear About:

- As you look at each measure, realize each note represents a sound. The number of notes in the measure tells you the number of sounds you will play or sing. So, in Exercise 1,

The GuitarPrinciples Path: Level One- Chords & Rhythm
Rhythm Four

- there is one sound (one strum) per measure. In Exercise 2, there are two sounds (strums) in the second measure.

- Even though the note symbol is in the middle of the measure, the sound starts right at the beginning, on beat one.

- The length of the note is represented by the value of the note symbol, not the physical distance between notes. Two eighth notes may be written with the same distance between them as two quarter notes, but the quarters are still sounding for twice as long as the eighths.

- I have left out the up arrows in parenthesis (↑) for clarity sake. Please realize that your hand comes up, with your foot, in between each down strum. The hand keeps a continuous motion with the foot.

Exercise 2: Whole and Half Notes

1. **Tap** foot, **count** out loud, saying counting symbols. **Whisper** the beats where no note is played.

2. **Tap** foot, **sing LA** for each note. So, Measure 1 has one sung LA lasting four beats. Measure 2 has two sung LA's, each lasting two beats.

3. **Tap** foot, **count** out loud, **strum** a chord where a note is played (bold numbers).

NOTE: Make sure as you count, you say 1 2 3 4. Many people mistakenly say 1 2 1 2. Don't forget, each beat has a separate counting symbol. For downbeats, it is the whole number.

Exercise 3: Whole, Half, and Quarter Notes

1. **Tap** foot, **count** out loud, saying counting symbols. Whisper the beats where no note is played.

2. **Tap** foot, **sing LA** for each note.

3. **Tap** foot, **count** out loud, **strum** a chord where a note is played (bold numbers).

Practice Approach Tip: If you feel a little shaky with these exercises, I strongly suggest that you take a piece of paper and write out some exercises based on those given here. Repetition on a variety of exercises will lead to mastery, and writing them yourself will enable you to internalize the knowledge better.

New Information: eighth notes can be written in two different ways. One way is to use a flag on an individual note:

Here are two eighth notes, each with a flag attached to the stem of the note.

Here is another way of writing those eighth notes. We attach the two notes with a beam, and leave out the flags.

You may see four or even eight notes beamed together in this manner.

Exercise 4: When The Eighth Note Gets One Beat

1. **Tap** foot, **count** out loud, saying counting symbols. **Whisper** the beats where no note is played.

2. **Tap** foot, **sing LA** for each note.

3. **Tap** foot, **count** out loud, **strum** a chord on where a note is played (bold numbers).

Remember, when you see an 8 in the bottom of the time signature, it means the eighth note gets one beat. So, the quarter note gets two beats.

Exercise 5: Whole, Half, Quarter, and Eighth Notes

Here the quarter note gets one beat, so the eighth note, which always gets ½ of the time the quarter note gets, receives ½ beat. So, you will strum down on the downbeat (where the whole number is), and you will strum up when your foot comes up (on the "+").

There are no "+'s" written between two quarter notes, since there is no new note being played on the upbeat in between those notes. Strumming-wise, this means the pick does not sound the strings on those upbeats, but merely passes by them on the way back up.

1. **Tap** foot, **count** out loud, saying counting symbols. **Whisper** the beats where no note is played.

2. **Tap** foot, **sing LA** for each note.

3. **Tap** foot, **count** out loud, **strum** a chord where a note is played.

The GuitarPrinciples Path: Level One- Chords & Rhythm
Rhythm Four

PRACTICE TIP: If you keep stumbling on a measure, **STOP** and just work on that measure separately until you understand it and can do it easily. **DON'T keep going back to the beginning and tripping over the same spot!**

Exercise 6: More Eighth Notes Count & Tap

Exercise 7: Common Eighth Note Strumming Patterns in 4/4 Time

Each measure (a, b, and c) is a separate pattern, which may be used for part or all of a song in accompaniment.

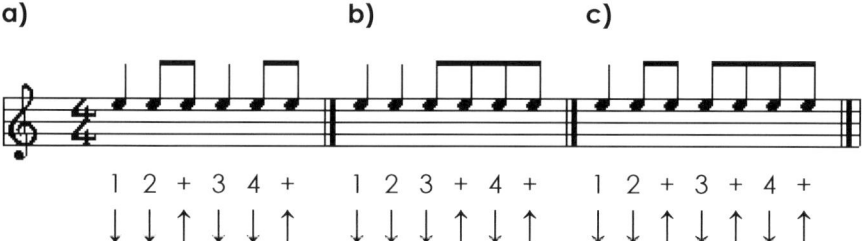

Exercise 8: Common Eighth Note Strumming Pattern in 3/4 Time

Remember, you must practice these until you can easily strum the chord to the correct rhythm while still tapping your foot and counting out loud. Being able to do so is proof that you have mind/body control and understanding of the rhythm. It will show in your playing.

Lesson Review: Key Points to Remember

When we say the counting symbols to a steadily tapping foot, it should sound like the rhythm of the notes they are written under, so we whisper the whole numbers that have no note above them. Also, we don't use "+'s" unless there is a note being sounded on that part of the beat (which is the middle of the beat, or upbeat).

Keep the hand in motion when strumming, even on "empty" beats, where you are not striking the strings.

If you keep having trouble with one measure of an exercise, stop and focus on that measure, going over it many times in a row, until it becomes easy. This may take several sessions over a few days.

THE GUITARPRINCIPLES PATH: RHYTHM FIVE

Exercises and Review

These are exercises for you to write in the counting symbols to various rhythms. If you can't do this, you don't understand what has been covered so far, and you must go back and review.

Guidelines: Remember the three questions you must ask, and be able to answer for each note.

1. **How many beats does this note get?** (e.g. this note gets ½ beat)

2. **What beats, or parts of beats, does it get?** (e.g. this note gets the second half of the second beat).

3. **What counting symbol is used to represent that beat or part of a beat?** (e.g. "+" is used to represent the second half of the second beat).

Whether to use a counting symbol or not: The downbeats, (when the foot is down) mark the beginning of one beat and the end of the previous one. <u>Downbeats ALWAYS have a counting symbol, a whole number, even if there is no note to go with it.</u>

In Exercise 2, where there is a half note in the first measure, getting beats 1 and 2, we write in the 2 even though there is no new note sounded on 2.

Other parts of the beat are only used if there is actually a note to go with them. <u>So, even though every quarter note has two parts, the first half and the second half, we only mark the second half with an "+" if there is actually a note sounded there.</u>

CORRECT

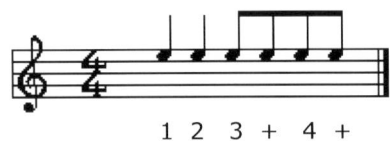

WRONG

The point here is that when we say the counting symbols to a steady beat (our foot), the saying of the counting symbols will give a representation of the rhythm of the notes. In other words, when you say the counting symbols to a steady beat, it sounds like the rhythm. So, except for the numbers marking all downbeats, (which we whisper when there is no note for it), the syllables of the counting symbols stand for a note being played

Instructions: **Write** in the counting symbols under each rhythm. Then, go back and **play** them, using a note or a chord. **Tap** your foot and **count** at the same time.

Last Tip: Remember, there are always the same amount of beats in a measure, but not always the same amount of notes. If the time signature is 4/4, every measure will have four beats (except possibly the first, which may be an incomplete measure containing "pick up notes"). But, a measure may contain NO notes, only silence (indicated by rests, explained in the next chapter), or the measure may have one note, or two, or many notes.

When you look at a measure, the number of notes tells you the number of separate sounds that will be made in that measure.

Exercise 1:

Exercise 2:

Exercise 3:

Exercise 4:

The GuitarPrinciples Path: Level One - Chords & Rhythm
Rhythm Five

Exercise 5:

Exercise 6:

Exercise 7:

Exercise 8:

Exercise 9:

THE GUITARPRINCIPLES PATH: RHYTHM SIX

Ties, Dots, Rests, and Syncopation

Ties

Sometimes we want a note that we are playing to last longer than is allowed by the number of beats in the measure. For instance, if we are playing a note on beat four of a measure in 4/4 time, we can only give that note one beat of time, beat four, since that is the last beat in the measure. But perhaps we want that particular note to last two beats. What do we do?

We do what all smart people do when they need something they don't have: we borrow it from our nearest neighbor! So, we borrow a beat from the next measure, and we do this by tying two notes together.

I would like this note to sound for two beats, but I have run out of beats in the measure

play   don't play   keep counting

So, I will "borrow" a beat's worth of time from the first beat of the next measure. I begin the note on beat four of the first measure, but I DO NOT PLAY ANOTHER NOTE ON THE FIRST BEAT OF THE NEXT MEASURE. Instead, I let the note I played on beat four of the first measure keep sounding until a new note is played on beat two of the second measure.

You will play the note on beat four, and keep counting, saying 1 for the first beat of the next measure, but do not play another note there. Instead, let the note played on beat four continue to ring.

So, in effect, the note I played on beat four of the first measure is sounding for two beats, like a half note, but it is written as a quarter note tied to another quarter note.

Rule for tied notes: Play the first note, don't play the second note, just keep counting, and let the first note ring.

Exercise 1: Ties In Various Time Signatures

Instructions: Write in the counting symbols. **Tap** your foot and **count** out loud as you **play**. Remember, you play the first note of a tied pair of notes, and DO NOT play the second note of a tied pair of notes, but let the first note sound for the duration of the second as well as the first.

a)

b)

c)

d)

Dots

A dot placed after a note is a short hand way of adding time to that note. Usually, a dot is explained as "increasing the value of the note by one half". I have found this definition to be very confusing to students. They often remember it as " a dot adds half a beat to a note", which is incorrect.

The real definition of what a dot does to a note is this: a dot increases a note's value by 50%. Whatever the note is worth, divide that value in half, and add it to the original value of the note.

So, if I have a half note in 4/4 time, it is worth two beats. If I dot that note, it will be worth its original value of two beats, as well as half of that, or one beat, for a total of three beats.

The GuitarPrinciples Path: Level One-Chords & Rhythm
Rhythm Six

1 2 3 4

If I have a quarter note in 4/4 time, it is worth one beat. If I dot that note, I am adding ½ of 1 to the original value. So, 1 + ½ equals a total of 1½ beats. Therefore, a dotted quarter note in 4/4 time is worth 1½ beats.

1 + 2 + 3 4

Now, we need to talk about the last example, the dotted quarter note in 4/4 time. This always causes students a lot of confusion, and we need to clear it up.

Again, remember the statement in Lesson Two: **In order to write in the counting symbols under the notes, you must be able to answer three questions for every note:**

1. **How many beats does this note get ?**

2. **Which beats does it get ?**

3. **What counting symbols are used to mark those beats or parts of beats ?**

For example, we may say: "this note gets two beats, and they are the first and second beats in the measure, marked by the counting symbols 1, 2.

We must be able to answer these questions for the example above. We must be able to say "the dotted quarter note gets 1½ beats. It gets all of the first beat and the first half of the second beat. Then, we must realize that the following eighth note gets the remaining 2nd half of the 2nd beat.

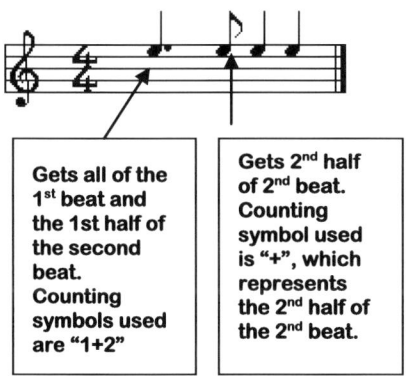

Gets all of the 1st beat and the 1st half of the second beat. Counting symbols used are "1+2"

Gets 2nd half of 2nd beat. Counting symbol used is "+", which represents the 2nd half of the 2nd beat.

Now, we must understand how to write in the counting symbols for these notes. Usually, when asked to write the counting symbols in for a dotted quarter note, the student will write "1 +" under the dotted quarter note. This is WRONG!

The root of this misunderstanding lies in the fact that when we first learn about quarter notes, and how they get one beat, we begin to associate the whole numbers with whole beats. Thus "1" symbolizes ALL of the first beat, "2" symbolizes ALL of the second beat, and they DO symbolize all of the beat when used for quarter notes, as in the example below.

1 2 3 4.....................**Each whole number represents a whole beat.**

But when we are dividing the beat in half, and using the counting symbols "1+2+" **the whole number no longer represents the whole beat.** It represents only the first half of the beat. The "+" represents the other half of the beat. This fact must be consciously recognized.

1 + 2 + 3 4 ....the whole numbers represent only the first half of the beat now. The "+" represents the second half.

So, we must understand that the dotted quarter note in 4/4 time gets 1½ beats, and <u>three counting symbols are required to represent that 1½ beats</u>. Each of those counting symbols "1+2" represents by itself one half beat.

The Behavior of the Foot on Dotted Quarter Notes in 4/4 Time

It always takes some careful practice to learn dotted quarter notes in 4/4 time and feel comfortable with them. Since they are usually followed by a single eighth note on the remaining half beat, we are required to play a note on that upbeat.

The fact that a note is NOT played on the downbeat, added to the fact that a note IS played on an upbeat, leads to a "floating" and unanchored kind of feeling that is a little strange at first. It's like jumping into the water for the first time when we learn to swim. But, knowing why it feels strange, and knowing what to do about it, will enable you to get very used to this sensation.

1   +   2   +

This is the path your foot takes when playing a dotted quarter note that starts on the downbeat. Your foot starts out down, goes up, comes back down, and goes up again. The single eighth note that follows begins when the foot is UP the second time, which is the beginning of the second half of the second beat.

Ex. 2: Dotted Quarters in 4/4 Time

Instructions:

1. Write in the counting symbols.

2. Write in arrows for your foot if necessary.

3. Tap foot, say counting symbols out loud in time with foot.

4. Tap foot, say "LA" in correct rhythm.

5. Tap foot, play the notes on guitar, say counting symbols out loud.

Remember, when you play the single eighth note, your foot should be UP, and you should be saying "and" (+). Also, play this note with an UP-PICK.

The GuitarPrinciples Path: Level One-Chords & Rhythm
Rhythm Six

Rests: Notating Silence

Music takes place in two dimensions: sound and time. The sound part is divided into two modes: sound, and the absence of sound, or silence. Like the sounds, the silence must be measured out time-wise, so that we know exactly how long to maintain silence. As usual, our unit of time is the beat.

For each type of note value, there is a corresponding symbol that tells us to be silent. So, a quarter note in 4/4 time means one beat of sound, and a quarter note rest means one beat of silence. Here are the rest symbols and their corresponding notes and values.

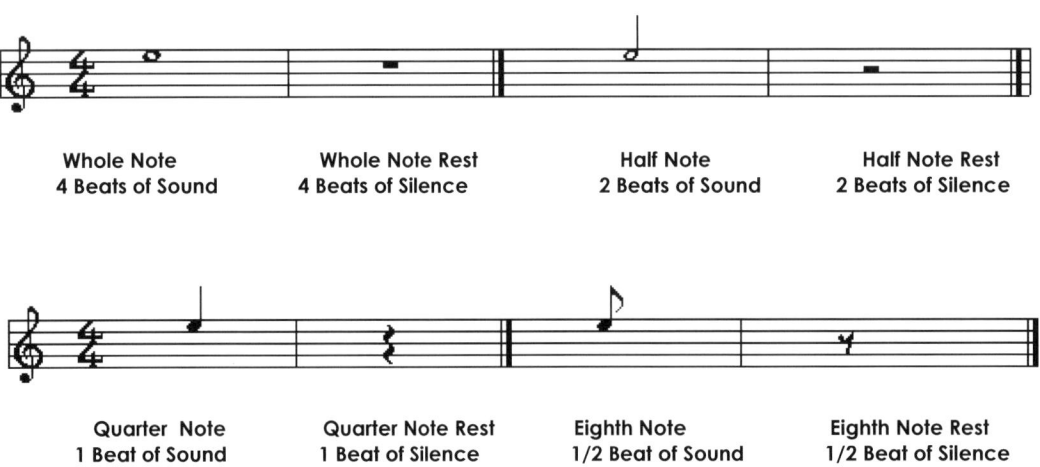

Whole Note — 4 Beats of Sound
Whole Note Rest — 4 Beats of Silence
Half Note — 2 Beats of Sound
Half Note Rest — 2 Beats of Silence

Quarter Note — 1 Beat of Sound
Quarter Note Rest — 1 Beat of Silence
Eighth Note — 1/2 Beat of Sound
Eighth Note Rest — 1/2 Beat of Silence

Exercise 3: Rests

Instructions:

1. **Write** in the counting symbols.

2. **Write** in arrows for your foot if necessary.

3. **Tap** foot, **say counting symbols** out loud in time with foot.

4. **Tap** foot, **say "LA"** in correct rhythm.

5. **Tap** foot, **play** notes on the guitar, **say counting symbols** out loud.

NOTE: Since we are playing an open string, we need to stop the sound when we get to the rest. When you get to the rest (beat 3 in measure 1, beat 2 in measure 2), stop the sound by lightly touching the string with a left-hand finger.

a)

b)

c)

d)

Syncopation: Accenting Weak Beats or the Weak Part of the Beat

In every measure of music, there are "weak" beats and "strong" beats. A strong beat is one that receives a natural accent, or we could say they are naturally stressed when played. The first beat of a measure is always strong.

The second beat is weak. The third beat is strong also, and the fourth beat is weak. If we put the accent on a naturally weak beat, such as 2 or 4, it creates that "floating" feeling I mentioned before, and this is called "syncopation".

Syncopation is the name given to the effect produced by accenting a weak beat, or a weak part of the beat.

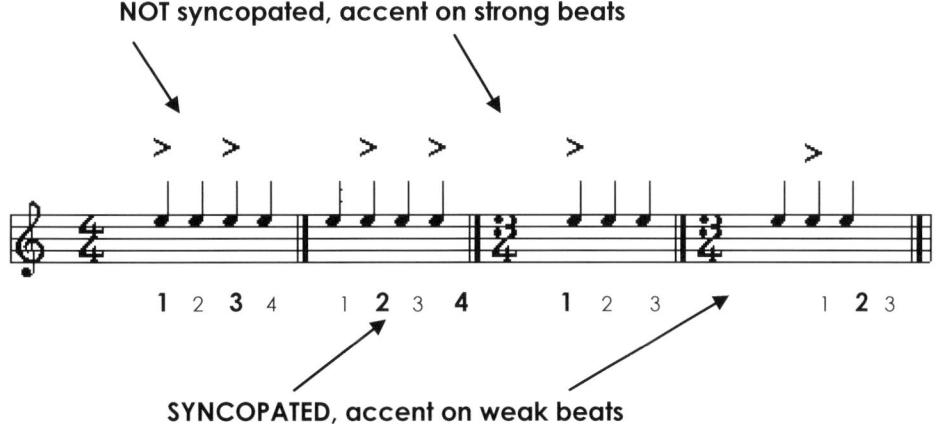

Tap and count the rhythms above, and say the accented beats louder to feel the syncopation. The second measure, by the way, is used in all rock music. On beats two and four, the snare drum is used to provide an accent on these weak beats, creating a constant syncopated effect called the **"backbeat"**.

Now, let's talk about the weak and strong PARTS of the beat. We talked before about downbeats and upbeats. Downbeats are strong, upbeats are weak. If we put the accent on the upbeat, we create syncopation.

The downbeat is STRONG　　　　　　　　　　**The upbeat is WEAK**

The most common way of accenting a weak beat or a weak part of the beat and thereby create syncopation, is to leave out the strong beat or the downbeat. This can be done with a tie, or a dot, or a rest.

In the previous exercises, we have created syncopation with dots and rests, as when we did this:

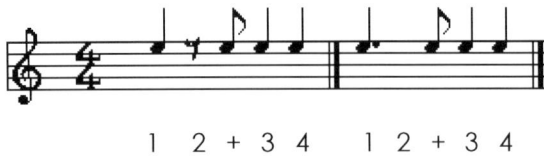

1 2 + 3 4　　1 2 + 3 4

In the first measure, the eighth note rest creates a "hole" on the downbeat, and the eighth note following is thereby accented, creating syncopation. In the second measure, the dotted quarter note lasts through the second beat, and no new note is struck (attacked) on the second beat.

So, the following eighth note on the upbeat creates syncopation.

New Information: Meter

There are two ways of grouping notes together, according to how we accent beats. The first way is called Duple Meter.

Duple meter means grouping the notes so that one beat is strong, the next is weak.

The GuitarPrinciples Path: Level One-Chords & Rhythm
Rhythm Six

Duple Meter is Strong-Weak. 2/4 time is duple, so is 4/4 time (two groups of Strong-Weak)

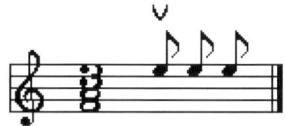

Triple Meter is Strong-Weak-Weak.

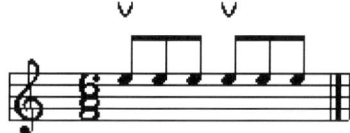

Exercise 4: Creating Syncopation with Ties

<u>Instructions:</u>

1. Write in the counting symbols.

2. Write in arrows for your foot if necessary.

3. Tap foot, say counting symbols out loud in time with foot. On the tied note where the note is not struck, whisper the counting symbol.

4. Tap foot, say counting symbols, and play the notes as notes or strums.

NOTE: You may find it helpful to also practice tapping the foot and saying the direction of the strum, as in "Down-Down-Up----Up-Down" for the first measure.

71

The GuitarPrinciples Path: Level One-Chords & Rhythm
Rhythm Six

a)
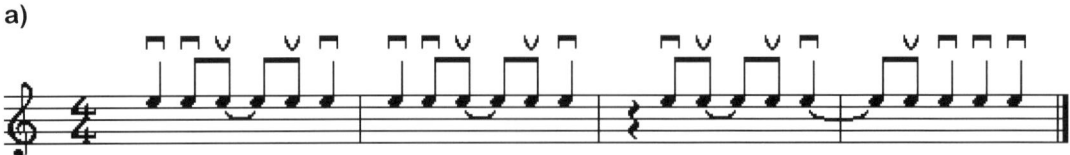

b)

Common Strumming Patterns

These strumming patterns can be used to play thousands of songs. However, don't forget that a simple quarter note strum is often the most effective accompaniment to a song, as well as a simple alternate bass.

Master these patterns, and apply them to many songs.

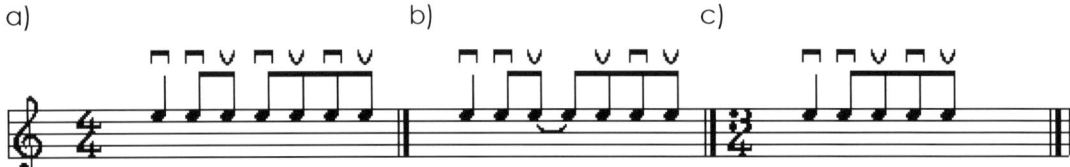

Lesson Review: Key Definitions & Concepts

Tie: a curved line that connects two notes. The first one is sounded, the second one is not. The time value of the second one is added to the first.

Dot: a dot placed after the head of the note increases the time value of the note by 50%.

Rests: periods of time in which there is no sound are represented by "rests". Each type of note has a corresponding rest symbol, that tells us to keep silent for the time value of the corresponding note value.

Syncopation: accenting a weak beat or a weak part of the beat.

Strong Beats & Weak Beats: the first beat in a measure is always strong. Two and four are weak beats in 4/4 time. Two and three are weak in ¾ time. The downbeat is always strong, the upbeat is weak.

Meter: the way beats are grouped is called meter. There are two kinds of meter: Duple: groups of two, and triple: groups of three. Other meters are extensions of these two.

Dotted Quarter Notes: When writing in the counting symbols for dotted quarter notes, three counting symbols must be used under the note. When we write in the counting symbols under whole beats (as in quarter notes in 4/4 time), the whole number represents the whole beat. However, when the beat is divided, as in eighth notes in 4/4 time, the whole number represents only the first half of the beat, the "+" represents the second half of the beat.

THE GUITAR PRINCIPLES PATH: RHYTHM SEVEN

Sixteenth Notes When the Quarter Note Gets One Beat

What are sixteenth notes?

We have divided the beat in half, and learned that in 4/4 time, the eighth note gets ½ beat. Now, we are going to divide the beat into quarters. A sixteenth note is worth ½ the time value of an eighth note, so, since an eighth note is worth ½ beat in 4/4 time, a sixteenth note is worth ¼ beat in 4/4 time.

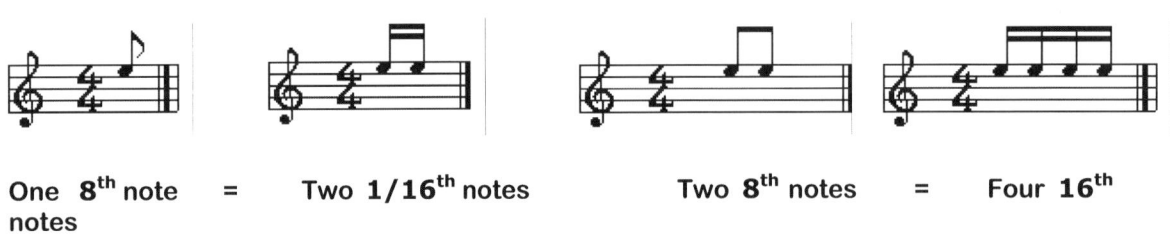

One 8th note　　=　　Two 1/16th notes　　　　Two 8th notes　　=　　Four 16th notes

The Position of the Foot for Sixteenth Notes

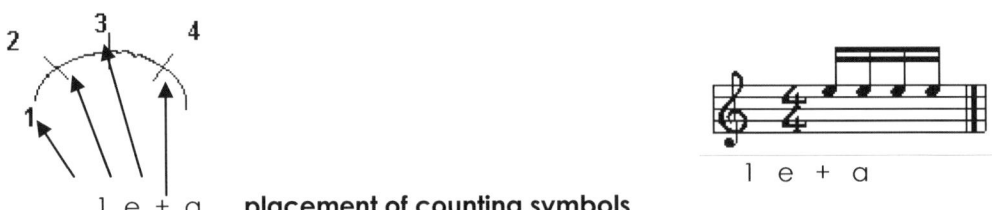

placement of counting symbols

Here is the beat divided into quarters. The numbers show the position of your foot; where it will be as each of the four sixteenth notes in a measure is played. Next, we see the counting symbols used to count the four sixteenth notes, 1 e + a.

- "1"　(or whatever beat number we are on) is the first sixteenth note.
- "e"　is the second sixteenth in the group.
- "+"　is the third sixteenth note. This is the middle of the beat, the same as before, when we first divided the beat for eighth notes.
- "a"　is the last sixteenth note, the fourth one.

When we play and tap eighth notes, it is easy to tell when the foot is all the way up, which marks the middle of the beat, and is where we say "and". However, in sixteenth notes, it is not so easy to tell when the foot is halfway up, or halfway down. So, in order to place the second and fourth notes of a sixteenth note group accurately in place time-wise, we rely on saying "1 e + a" in a smooth way, so that the syllables are evenly spaced. Then, we play the notes in the same smooth way.

So, make sure when you count sixteenth notes you say "1 e + a" evenly, not "1 e   + a" or something like that. If this is all totally new to you, the most foolproof way of counting out sixteenth notes is to put the metronome on 100, and count "1 e + a" using one counting symbol for each click, but having the foot go down only on the whole number, or every fifth click.

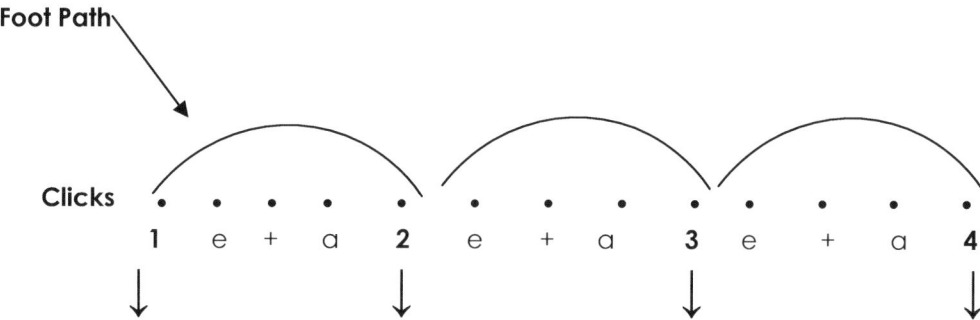

You have a click for every sixteenth note when you do this. After doing this, eliminate the clicks in between by putting the metronome on a slow setting like 50, tap only on the click, and say "1 e + a, 2 e + a", etc.

Remember, your foot will go down on the numbers, and you will say the counting symbols "1 e + a" evenly spaced throughout the time it takes for your foot to travel.

Switching Gears Between Note Values

It can be a little tricky at first to go from counting quarters and eighths to counting sixteenth notes. It feels like "switching gears" as you go from "1, 2, 3, 4" to "1+2+3+4+", to "1e+a 2e+a 3e+a 4e+a". But, practice is the answer, of course.

Exercise 1: Quarters, Eighths, and Sixteenth Notes

INSTRUCTIONS: Tap, count out loud, and play. If you have trouble, put the metronome on 100, and take four clicks for the quarter note, two for the eighth note, and one for each sixteenth note. This way, by giving the smallest note value its own click as a marker, you will know exactly where each note is supposed to be.

After getting comfortable, try it with one click per quarter on a slower beat, around 50.

a)

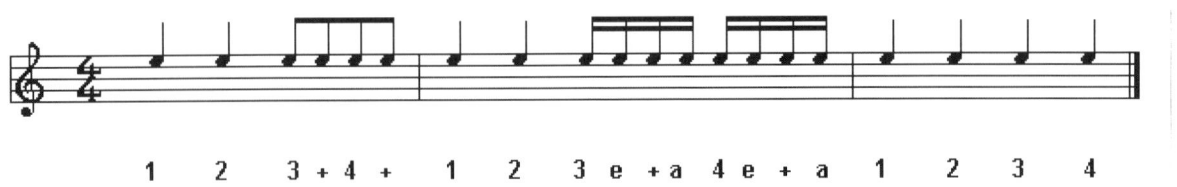

b)

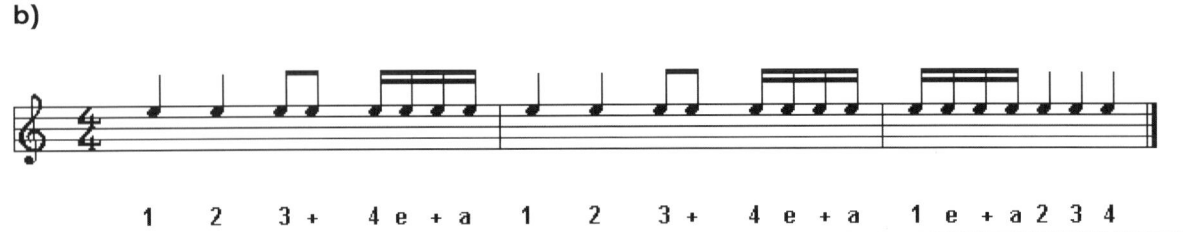

Other Sixteenth Note Groupings

In addition to four sixteenths in a row, you will frequently encounter a few other sixteenth note groupings. Here are some examples below. (They contain only one beat in the measure, not four.)

Again, the most foolproof way of learning these rhythms is to put the metronome on 100, and count "1 e + a" using one counting symbol for each click, but having the foot go down only on the whole number, or every fifth click. For each rhythm, leave out the counting symbols that have no note to go with them.

So, for Exercise A, don't say the "e", but leave the space of course. For Exercise B, don't say the "a". Exercise "C" is tricky, you have to leave out the middle of the beat, the "+".

Work on these next examples and master them. Keep doing them, if only a few minutes a day, and as the days go by, you will get comfortable with them.

Exercise 2: Other Common Sixteenth Note Groups

Instructions: **Write** in the counting symbols, **tap, count**, and **play**. If you have trouble, follow the same instructions given.

Common Sixteenth Note Strumming Patterns

NOTE: Just in case you don't know yet, the symbols for a down pick or up pick are as shown below. I will use them also to indicate down or up strum in the following rhythms.

The Guitar Principles Path: Level One-Chords & Rhythm
Rhythm Seven

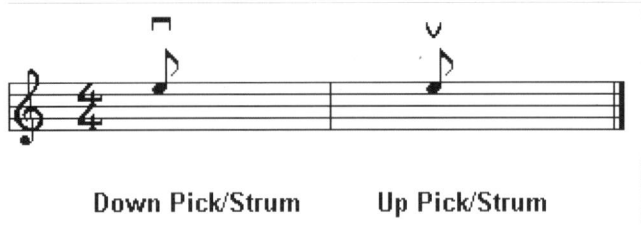

Down Pick/Strum   **Up Pick/Strum**

INSTRUCTIONS: Strum these rhythm patterns using the up and down strums as indicated.

a)

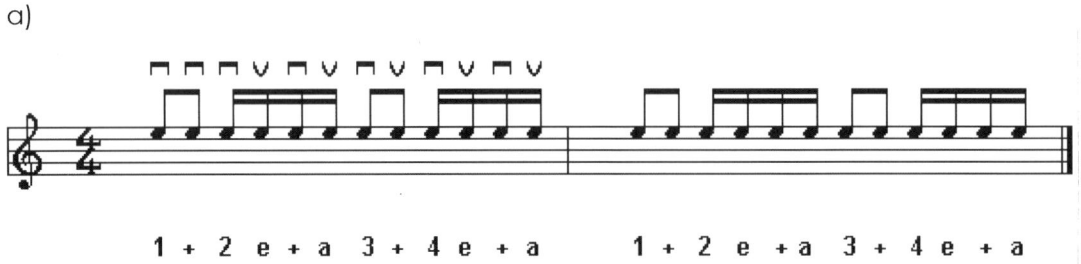

b)   Write in the counting symbols yourself on this one.

And the beat goes on................

Now you have all the knowledge and understanding you need to deal with most of the rhythms you will come into contact with. If you encounter anything more complex than what you have learned here, you will be able to figure it out by using what you have learned here, and perhaps consulting other resources.

Remember that it takes a good deal of practice and experience to feel comfortable in dealing with rhythm notation, so keep reviewing the material, and most especially, keep applying the knowledge with new exercises.

I suggest you make a regular habit of taking various pieces of music you happen to come across, and writing in the counting symbols under the notes, and singing or playing the rhythms just as we have done here. It will get easier and easier, and soon you will be a fluent interpreter of rhythm notation.